MERRIAM-WEBSTER'S

WORD PUZZLE ADVENTURES

Merriam-Webster Kids is an imprint of Merriam-Webster Inc., published in collaboration with What on Earth Publishing.

First published in the United States in 2022
Text copyright © 2022 Merriam-Webster Inc.
Illustrations copyright © 2022 Merriam-Webster Inc.

Developed by What on Earth Publishing

Written by Gabrielle Vernon-Melzer
Illustrated by Sam Rennocks
Designed by Jo Garden
Edited by Priyanka Lamichhane
Print and Production Consultancy by Booklabs.co.uk

Staff for this book
Merriam-Webster Inc.: Linda Wood, Senior Editor;
Em Vezina, Director of Editorial Operations

What on Earth Publishing: Nancy Feresten, Publisher;
Natalie Bellos, Editorial Director; Meg Osborne, Assistant Editor;
Andy Forshaw, Art Director; Nell Wood, Designer

Library of Congress Cataloging-in-Publication Data available upon request
First Edition, 2022
ISBN: 9780877791447
TC/Quebec, Canada/08/2022
Printed in Canada

10 9 8 7 6 5 4 3 2 1

MERRIAM-WEBSTER'S

WORD PUZZLE ADVENTURES

Track down dinosaurs, uncover
treasures, spot the space objects,
and learn about language!

Merriam-Webster kids

CONTENTS

HOW TO USE THIS BOOK

Pencils ready! This book is packed with ingenious puzzles for you to scribble on and figure out. Here are some pointers to get you started.

 You'll find **WORD SEARCHES** on all sorts of exciting topics, from astronomy to ice cream flavors, and from desert animals to flying machines. To find the words, search across, down, and diagonally.

```
L A O N I Y D A A I L N L A L
C A N D A C R O S S N I N A N
C L D A I R L W G S A A R I W
Y C O R O A C Y G S S A A L L
N D O A C S G N W N L O D L L
G N Y O A L A O Y A C N N A I
O D A S A A L I N L N G A G Y
Y D L A A O A O Y A C A O D S
D O O R D R L N D S L A G D W
N W N O D S O L S A A L A G A
L N A R O S N A S R N D Y R L
L O D C C C O S D S A R A L D
N D W C A L O S S S A A A O Y
A D S O W L O Y N O D O A Y Y
L S O D I A N N S O S L C D O
```

Discover **WORD MAGICIAN PUZZLES**, where you switch letters to conjure a new word. For example, by changing one letter, WORD becomes WOOD, becomes HOOD, becomes HOOP.

W O R D

CLUE: Furniture might be made of this

W   O   _O_   D

CLUE: Something that covers your head

_H_   _O_   _O_   _D_

CLUE: A circular object or ring

_H_   _O_   _O_   _P_

 Smarten up with **WORD WHIZ QUIZZES** full of interesting and unusual words that will ELEVATE your vocabulary.

To lift up or improve something

And these aren't the only puzzles in this book. You'll discover crosswords, fill-in-the-blank games, word scrambles, and quizzes about Earth, space, and everything in between.

Ready to get started? LET'S GO!

INTO THE RAINFOREST

Can you spy the 10 rainforest animals?

```
L L L A L P I A O L A G E L L
B S F G R S A N A R P P R A I
R O I R B F H R A N R O A B D
Y N M O I U L H R A G O G R O
A L T F L A D L L O N T D O O
G I B B O N H L E O T O B P I
U U A R D G I S U M O R F L C
T E L R A R O L O J U F U A C
G O R I L L A O U A C R R O A
Y R A A A O G T F G A A E O O
O O O U A A C H L U N G I R G
A L G O A O G A N A C O N D A
P E A A T T F R H R T L A N I
H S L B U T T E R F L Y O R L
P A L S O C O A O A B O M A O
```

- ☐ GORILLA
- ☐ BUTTERFLY
- ☐ SLOTH
- ☐ TOUCAN
- ☐ PARROT
- ☐ JAGUAR
- ☐ GIBBON
- ☐ LEMUR
- ☐ ANACONDA
- ☐ FROG

DESERT
DISCOVERIES

Find these 10 desert-dwelling creatures.

```
L E O T A R M R S E T O
R T P M E E E U A E E I
A M E I R N E A N M H D
L E K A O S R N D O C D
H A R E L E K I C D N K
E Y N S R A A H A A C A
O O E C E C T Y T E R R
C S I O I E O A S K J M
E I Y R A S A C E W R A
E D A P T A I O A S E D
M E E I T E D Y D M I I
R W E O N A O O O R E L
R I E N A N A T E A E L
I N D A E E T E D R E O
N D P O J E R B O A R C
I E O H S A R D E E R D
D R R O A D R U N N E R
```

- ☐ SCORPION
- ☐ CAMEL
- ☐ COYOTE
- ☐ SIDEWINDER
- ☐ MEERKAT
- ☐ ROADRUNNER
- ☐ JERBOA
- ☐ HARE
- ☐ SAND CAT
- ☐ ARMADILLO

DID YOU KNOW?

SIDEWINDERS are snakes! They earned their name because of the way they side-shuffle to move themselves along the sand.

Answers on page 112

WILD OCEAN

Unscramble the letters to name 5 ocean-dwelling animals.

N G I E P N U

_ _ _ _ _ _ _

 L O N I D P H

_ _ _ _ _ _ _

A H E S E O R S

_ _ _ _ _ _ _ _

B C R A

_ _ _ _

 Q I D U S

_ _ _ _ _

WORD MAGICIAN

Change the letters to create new words.

CHANGE ONE LETTER TO MAKE THE NEXT WORD : M A P S

CLUE: These items help clean the floor   M _ P S

CLUE: What a bunny does   _ _ _ _

CLUE: What a balloon does when it breaks   _ _ _ _

CLUE: Young dogs   _ _ _ _

CHANGE TWO LETTERS TO MAKE THE NEXT WORD : L A N E

CLUE: You might whistle this   _ _ N E

CLUE: Means the same as "finished"   _ _ _ _

CLUE: Comes before "ten"   _ _ _ _

CLUE: Thoughtful and sweet   _ _ _ _

    Answers on page 112

LITTLE FRIENDS

Add the baby animal names to the crossword.

ACROSS

4. A baby horse

5. A baby pig

7. A baby kangaroo

8. A baby snake

9. A baby swan

DOWN

1. A baby dog

2. A baby frog

3. A baby cat

6. A baby duck

9. A baby cow

WORD BANK

- [ ] FOAL
- [ ] PIGLET
- [ ] JOEY
- [ ] SNAKELET
- [ ] CYGNET
- [ ] PUPPY
- [ ] TADPOLE
- [ ] KITTEN
- [ ] DUCKLING
- [ ] CALF

ANIMAL EXPERT

How much do you know about baby animals?

(Hint: You can find all answers in the crossword opposite!)

1 Which gray-feathered baby animal grows up to become a beautiful white bird?

_ _ _ _ _ _

2 This barnyard animal is born very small, but can weigh up to 700 pounds as an adult.

_ _ _ _ _ _

3 When this animal is a baby, it has a special tooth that helps it break its shell and hatch from its egg.

_ _ _ _ _ _ _ _

4 What animal is born fluffy but grows up to have waterproof feathers?

_ _ _ _ _ _ _ _

5 Which baby animal sleeps in its mother's pouch?

_ _ _ _

Answers on page 112

TOWERING TREES

Find the names of 10 trees in this forest of letters.

```
O L L R R G Y R D C Y W L
R O G C H E R R Y E M O O
S R T D O O M O R L L W O
D S Y C A M O R E W O I M
A D A A R R C D M A E L R
R E V E R G R E E N O L E
E W O C H E S T N U T O N
E O A E O E V N W I O W L
L D K E M A P L E W O T V
Y O L O H R N O R Y L M M
R P V L G E L K G E O P A
G E W Y K D E N R A V E G
L D D S R W R L E G M N N
A O D H N O A K R E E M O
O D H W D O G W O O D L L
W C I E T D K O G L E M I
R H W W G A D R Y D N G A
```

- [ ] WILLOW
- [ ] REDWOOD
- [ ] MAPLE
- [ ] DOGWOOD
- [ ] EVERGREEN
- [ ] CHERRY
- [ ] MAGNOLIA
- [ ] CHESTNUT
- [ ] OAK
- [ ] SYCAMORE

FABULOUS FLOWERS

Can you sniff out the 10 flowers hidden below?

```
D F U W T S F D R U E O T U O O L
R L E H R L T U V I O L E T D C C
D C Y K O L N O O F O R H I A H E
S W D E D L A V T E D V O R F E Y
S E L S U N F L O W E R N S F R O
U C R F H S O H B P R K E I O R O
L T A T R F R O Y C E O Y I D Y U
E R D D U W B O L H E R S R I B M
E U A P E L I F F E R S U E L L T
R V I D O E I T U E U L C R L O T
N O S F E K C P R D E E K B P S Y
H A Y M E W C H O Y R I L O O S S
O S I E I I I D L U K A E R T O I
D P E R I W I N K L E S L T I M T
B U T T E R C U P O T I S E M T M
U S E B A Y A I E U S E M L B D E
```

- ☐ DAFFODIL
- ☐ HONEYSUCKLE
- ☐ ROSE
- ☐ DAISY
- ☐ SUNFLOWER
- ☐ TULIP
- ☐ VIOLET
- ☐ BUTTERCUP
- ☐ PERIWINKLE
- ☐ CHERRY BLOSSOM

Answers on page 113

WORD WHIZ

Find all 8 wacky words.

☐ LABRADOODLE
☐ BLUNDER
☐ SUPERNOVA
☐ SQUABBLE
☐ INFINITY
☐ DOLLOP
☐ HULLABALOO
☐ OMNIVORE

```
Y S L P O S D O R H R O E E R O
Q B D I L N O L I U A I T T A P
L B N I O O A L Q L V U B O O L
N A D N D L L S B L S V E N B I
Y U B T O D I U N A Q O B I R E
D A L R N B N P B B U O L P A O
E B D A A T R E E A A O O U B O
P U O I Y D I R D L B R A V R A
O U T Q A O O N S O B O D U O F
M A E B B L I O O O L L U N O O
N E B N E B A V D O E L Q H E A
I L D U O O O A N L U U O L N E
V N D A R B L U N D E R F P E I
O D Y N D E B O I I S U O O L Y
R I N F I N I T Y B B D S L E L
E O M E U T O A R N L B O D I R
```

WORD WHIZ QUIZ

Can you match each word to its definition?

HULLABALOO

INFINITY

DOLLOP

OMNIVORE

SUPERNOVA

LABRADOODLE

BLUNDER

SQUABBLE

A loud, continued noise or mixture of noises

An animal that eats both plants and meat

A dog that is a cross between a Labrador retriever and a poodle

A spoonful of something soft or mushy

An exploding star

A silly mistake

An unlimited space, amount, or period of time

A fight over something that is not important

Answers on page 113

COME ONE, COME ALL!

Crack circus-themed clues to complete the crossword.

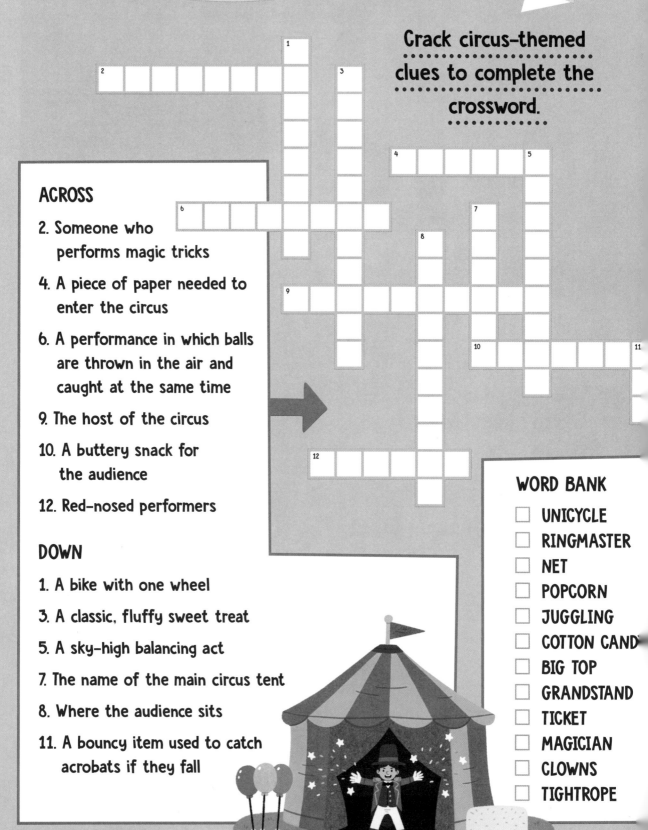

ACROSS

2. Someone who performs magic tricks
4. A piece of paper needed to enter the circus
6. A performance in which balls are thrown in the air and caught at the same time
9. The host of the circus
10. A buttery snack for the audience
12. Red-nosed performers

DOWN

1. A bike with one wheel
3. A classic, fluffy sweet treat
5. A sky-high balancing act
7. The name of the main circus tent
8. Where the audience sits
11. A bouncy item used to catch acrobats if they fall

WORD BANK

- ☐ UNICYCLE
- ☐ RINGMASTER
- ☐ NET
- ☐ POPCORN
- ☐ JUGGLING
- ☐ COTTON CANDY
- ☐ BIG TOP
- ☐ GRANDSTAND
- ☐ TICKET
- ☐ MAGICIAN
- ☐ CLOWNS
- ☐ TIGHTROPE

Answers on page 113

WORD MAGICIAN

Change the letters to create new words.

CHANGE ONE LETTER TO MAKE THE NEXT WORD	:	S O U P

CLUE: What you use to wash your hands   S O _ P

CLUE: To fly through the sky   _ _ _ _

CLUE: How a lemon tastes   _ _ _ _

CLUE: There are 60 minutes in one of these   _ _ _ _

CHANGE TWO LETTERS TO MAKE THE NEXT WORD	:	B O O K

CLUE: Backyard swimming spot   _ O O _

CLUE: The opposite of push   _ _ _ _

CLUE: What you do with a telephone   _ _ _ _

CLUE: Where bats often hang out   _ _ _ _

Answers on page 113

TIME FOR ACTION!

Find all 10 "doing" words hidden in this word search.

```
T A S T E S A E E E R U
S S R A S T I P T O E S
J U G G L E E L T E H I
E C S S E H U C L L E S
T T R W H I S T L E A W
J G L U W T L S H D R U
C S U L D I S C U S S O
A A R L W U R G E I E S
S U L H A R E L E E E O
E P S C L B S A G W R E
E U H S U E W E T E U S
E S P T T L T C E L P G
P T E R R L A H W I T G
W U R E S O H T A C H W
L A H T C W T P E U D P
C J S C O H A T S A T R
H S E H C E A O S U S S
```

- ☐ TIPTOE
- ☐ BELLOW
- ☐ JUGGLE
- ☐ CALCULATE
- ☐ REHEARSE
- ☐ DISCUSS
- ☐ ERUPT
- ☐ STRETCH
- ☐ WHISTLE
- ☐ WASH

DID YOU KNOW?

Action words are called VERBS.

QUICKLY, SLOWLY

DID YOU KNOW? These words are called ADVERBS. Adverbs describe actions.

Can you find these 10 words that end in "ly"?

```
U S T E E S S Y Y E S A E L Y L
L A C L E A F U O I L C Y E I E
Y L Y E F Y L O Y N E S E F O S
R S E B E E F O O E O E H L I
S I I B R O F E R L P C I A E L
V P E C M A P E E I I P E P T E
E Q E I R I V E R Q L S S P I N
O U S P U E C E S I Y O H I A T
E I P P R A E L L E L R T L L
N E I Y S I M P L Y N L P Y Y Y
L T I Y R F L F I E R C E L Y L
I L F E Y L E Y E L L R O I Y B
N Y N B N T Y A P H Y Y E Y L A
L Y Y F O R T U N A T E L Y L L
L I U Y N E A E L I Y B L F Y L
```

☐ SIMPLY   ☐ BRAVELY   ☐ HAPPILY
☐ CREEPILY   ☐ QUIETLY   ☐ FORTUNATELY
☐ SLEEPILY   ☐ FIERCELY
☐ FOOLISHLY   ☐ SILENTLY

21

Answers on page 114

IT'S A RAINBOW!

Find 7 color words to make a rainbow.

```
Y B V I O L E T I L O I N E E
N L Y Y N E R G R R E E O T L
B L U E E D E E O D B A R B E
G R L O L O I Y I L E R U W R
E E Y E E L G G L I Y T E E E
W V L L A N O N O R L E R E D
A D O E D G L W W L W R E O G
O B R U E T E L I R E I I I Y
O U A O O L E Y E N U R O E E
G E N L L N L W R B I N R E D
E R G E R O R A G L O E L L O
E I E R N V O D T E R E N R A
R I N E E I V I E E O R E R O
L N T E B E O O G A G T R L O
U N O O E L N N D B U L N U L
```

- [ ] RED
- [ ] ORANGE
- [ ] YELLOW
- [ ] GREEN
- [ ] BLUE
- [ ] INDIGO
- [ ] VIOLET

WILD WEATHER

Fill in the missing vowels to create weather words.

A E I O U

BL_ZZ_RD

SN_W

CL__DY

L_GHTN_NG

SL__T

R__N

H__TW_V_

TH_ND_R

H__L

T_RN_D_

Answers on page 114

STAR CHART

Hey, stargazer!
Can you find
8 constellations?

```
R O R O D D G D E N I R P V E
U S D A B I I G R M D B A M E
I B U Y N A V B R A D A A R D
D R N I T S P B D R R R U A I
O N G H N A G R U N I R E B I
R I R Y P R U E R U E I M I R
N E R D T R A R I E S A A G E
R A V R T N A R U I R R H D R
S U I A R S D A R S R G D I P
I N R I R T A E P A S E I P I
P S G S S N N A H N G M D P N
M O O R I O N B E U E I O E G
M G A N D R O M E D A N G R M
T R T A V R A G O I A I E I V
D N A R N I P R N I I A N S G
```

☐ TAURUS   ☐ HYDRA
☐ BIG DIPPER   ☐ GEMINI
☐ ORION   ☐ ANDROMEDA
☐ ARIES   ☐ VIRGO

SECRET STELLAR CODES

Solve these "backward" codes to learn
some facts about stars!

RATS A SI NUS EHT
THE SUN IS A STAR

SAG GNINRUB FO EDAM ERA SRATS

_ _ _ _ _   _ _ _   _ _ _ _   _ _
_ _ _ _ _ _ _   _ _ _

SEIXALAG DELLAC SPUORG NI DNUOF ERA SRATS

_ _ _ _ _   _ _ _   _ _ _ _   _ _   _ _ _ _ _
_ _ _ _ _ _   _ _ _ _ _ _ _ _

EULB ERA SRATS TSETTOH EHT

_ _ _   _ _ _ _ _ _ _   _ _ _ _ _   _ _   _ _ _ _

YAW YKLIM EHT DELLAC SI YXALAG RUO

_ _ _   _ _ _ _ _   _ _   _ _ _ _ _
_ _ _   _ _ _ _ _   _ _ _

Answers on page 114

SUPER SLEUTH

Do you know what these words mean?
Circle the correct answer.

1 GORGONZOLA is ...

A   a type of cheese

B   a type of boat found in Venice

2 AILUROPHOBIA is ...

A   a fear of cats

B   a fear of boats

3 An ARTICHOKE is ...

A   a vegetable

B   a beautiful scarf

4 An OCTAGON is ...

A   a sea creature

B   a shape

5 A EWE is ...

A   a sheep

B   something that tastes disgusting

6 A MOLAR is ...

A   a tooth

B   a burrowing animal

7 A LIAR is ...

A a person who doesn't tell the truth

B someone who sleeps all the time

8 A TEMPEST is ...

A someone with a fever

B a violent storm

9 A TARSIER is ...

A a sticky black liquid

B a nocturnal animal with big eyes

10 A SILHOUETTE is ...

A the outline of something

B a type of owl

11 A SHAMROCK is ...

A a crystal

B a plant

BUSY BODY

Thumbs up if you can find these 8 body words.

```
K A L A F O C L O T N G E
E B E A N A T T O O B A O
O D F L C K E U B N L I T
E T E B O A L A B G O N W
E E N E E T B E O U T H I
F N K N A E O A G E R I B
L F A B R L W E C O N G E
F L F K L F F A N K E R L
F O O T O O A R K A E L O
A R L K B B K H O A I L F
L F O R E H E A D T N L O
L E T T A O T E E E E T N
O L K E E T A L A D N B L
A L L N T O O L A B R G A
I E E B I A L A O N O N K
A L A E A E W T E E A L F
A O T B N E L U U W W O E
```

- ☐ ELBOW
- ☐ FOREHEAD
- ☐ TOENAIL
- ☐ TONGUE
- ☐ EARLOBE
- ☐ FOOT
- ☐ BACK
- ☐ ANKLE

WORD MAGICIAN

Change the letters to create new words.

CHANGE ONE LETTER TO MAKE THE NEXT WORD

M O O N

CLUE: What a cow does

M O O _

CLUE: How you feel

_ _ _ _

CLUE: What you eat

_ _ _ _

CLUE: The opposite of bad

_ _ _ _

CHANGE TWO LETTERS TO MAKE THE NEXT WORD

S E E D

CLUE: The stuff you walk on at the beach

S _ _ D

CLUE: A small body of water

_ _ _ _

CLUE: Something that holds your ice cream

_ _ _ _

CLUE: The hair around a male lion's neck

_ _ _ _

Answers on page 115

SENSATIONAL!

Can you find all 10 words that describe how things feel?

```
W E C S H C Y C G P Y I C S S
H I N I R Y M H S O L P T P G
S C U Y S T U E O O S H O C P
P S Y S H H S W E P C G O I O
S C R A T C H Y Y Y H C Y Y I
H P M T T L Y H L S R Y H I N
Y C I M C Y M I C O O R Y Y T
O M I K N T M S H G O H P C Y
Y S D U Y U C O T G H S C U Y
G S C K L S R R C Y Y Y D D H
Y M N S Y P I C G S C S S D M
T O Y C U I S L I M Y D Y L P
C O Y S S M P M S I U I L Y I
S T Y T A Y Y Y E H O P O D U
I H I D W M H Y K T I H T S P
```

- [ ] CUDDLY
- [ ] SPIKY
- [ ] SCRATCHY
- [ ] CRISPY
- [ ] MUSHY
- [ ] SLIMY
- [ ] SOGGY
- [ ] POINTY
- [ ] CHEWY
- [ ] SMOOTH

STUCK TOGETHER

Can you find the compound words?

```
A P H M R R R W L R S E
D I H S Y R U A P H E S
R L C A E I R R W W Y E
R L L I F E S T Y L E A
S O S T L L I R W A C G
S W I A S A H Y A I R U
W C R O S S W A L K D L
E A A A B Y O R K E L L
A S T R A C E T R A C K
T E D Y R E H G K R U S
S G S A N G S B C A R K
H A R W Y S E D S A L A
I L A I A T O A W R I A
R E E P R K I L T I B Y
T E W L D W D M K A C S
D O L L H O U S E L O H
H P D I S H W A S H E R
```

- [ ] LIFESTYLE
- [ ] BARNYARD
- [ ] DOLLHOUSE
- [ ] DAYTIME
- [ ] SWEATSHIRT
- [ ] RACETRACK
- [ ] PILLOWCASE
- [ ] SEAGULL
- [ ] DISHWASHER
- [ ] CROSSWALK

Answers on page 115

FRUIT
BOWL

WORD BANK

☐ STRAWBERRY   ☐ PEACH
☐ APPLE   ☐ MANGO
☐ CHERRY   ☐ GRAPE
☐ BANANA   ☐ PEAR
☐ WATERMELON   ☐ KIWI

Unscramble the letters to make fruit salad.

A N B A A N   G A N M O

_ _ _ _ _ _   _ _ _ _ _

E R A P   C A P E H

_ _ _ _   _ _ _ _ _

H E R C R Y   P L E P A

_ _ _ _ _ _   _ _ _ _ _

W I I K   G P R A E

_ _ _ _   _ _ _ _ _

A L E T E N W O R M

_ _ _ _ _ _ _ _ _ _

R S W A T E R B Y R

_ _ _ _ _ _ _ _ _ _

BAKE SALE

DID YOU KNOW?

The word "cake" has been in use for more than 700 years and comes from the Vikings. They called it "kaka."

Find these 10 hidden baking words before they go in the oven.

```
T  I  R  I  E  I  O  O  B  K  R  T
C  R  R  S  K  K  N  S  T  C  B  I
G  N  P  R  B  R  O  W  N  I  E  S
E  O  T  L  R  R  S  S  E  T  E  E
S  P  R  I  N  K  L  E  S  B  S  K
F  C  T  S  U  G  W  I  E  A  N  P
C  R  F  T  H  E  O  K  R  T  D  K
A  A  R  O  E  O  P  A  S  T  R  Y
A  G  I  N  G  E  R  B  R  E  A  D
O  D  M  O  B  K  C  T  A  R  U  O
O  U  U  U  T  I  U  A  C  R  I  U
A  N  F  A  A  O  P  E  O  A  A  G
E  L  F  B  I  D  C  N  F  G  K  H
C  N  I  I  O  D  A  D  E  G  T  E
E  A  N  C  O  O  K  I  E  R  Y  R
I  Y  G  I  O  R  E  O  P  U  A  A
R  G  R  E  P  T  I  K  O  T  R  B
```

- ☐ BATTER
- ☐ CUPCAKE
- ☐ GINGERBREAD
- ☐ BROWNIES
- ☐ DOUGH
- ☐ SPRINKLES
- ☐ MUFFIN
- ☐ SHORTCAKE
- ☐ COOKIE
- ☐ PASTRY

Answers on page 115

IN-TENTS!

Solve the clues in this camping-themed crossword.

WORD BANK

- ☐ S'MORES
- ☐ CAMPFIRE
- ☐ BACKPACK
- ☐ STARGAZE
- ☐ SLEEPING BAG
- ☐ HIKE
- ☐ GHOST STORIES
- ☐ TENTS
- ☐ FLASHLIGHT

ACROSS

2. The ultimate camping treat—don't forget the graham crackers!
4. Activity to do at night during clear skies
5. Warm nighttime spot for marshmallow roasting
8. A camper's bed (two words)
9. A long walk through the woods

DOWN

1. Scary tales told around the fire (two words)
3. A place to keep your supplies
6. Tool for seeing in the dark
7. Where campers sleep

CAMPFIRE QUIZ

How much do you know
about the great outdoors?

1. When you "pitch" a tent, what are you doing?

A Throwing it away

B Setting it up

C Making it waterproof

D Cleaning it

2. What are the three ingredients to make s'mores?

A Pretzels, frosting, and chocolate

B Peanut butter, chocolate, and marshmallows

C Chocolate, marshmallows, and graham crackers

D Marshmallows, caramel, and bread

3. What is a hammock?

A A type of hiking snack

B A quick-drying raincoat

C A huge backpack

D A swinging bed tied between two trees

4. Which structure are you likely to find on a campsite?

A Log cabin

B Igloo

C Apartment complex

D Mansion

Answers on page 116

WORD WHIZ

Find all 10 wonderful words.

- ☐ ZEST
- ☐ VOCABULARY
- ☐ UKULELE
- ☐ YUMMY
- ☐ SQUAWK
- ☐ RANDOM
- ☐ PARKA
- ☐ SLUMBER
- ☐ NICKEL
- ☐ PUDDLE

```
B U Z A U D Y U I Q Z Y A L B
L L A R A D P U D D L E V E V
K Z M R E E L D U L U N O Q P
E A R K P A R K A V U L C R S
S Q U A W K N L R S A U A M N
M U C M M E E I A E K D B M S
P E U A A D Y E C U L E U N L
R E L E I S N D S K D K L V W
A D U A B C L N U R E B A E P
N R B B K Q T U M T Y L R D M
D Y U A L L Z U M S E U Y V A
O A C Z D A N L Z B Z C M D R
M B K V U K U L E L E L U M A
L R P Y C C A R S N P R R U Y
U U E O D U L U T E D A A U M
```

WORD WHIZ QUIZ

Can you match each word to its definition?

UKULELE

ZEST

PARKA

NICKEL

PUDDLE

VOCABULARY

RANDOM

An exciting quality

Great-tasting

Without a clear pattern

A warm, windproof winter coat

A short, harsh cry often made by birds

A collection of words and their meanings

A small instrument similar to a guitar

A five-cent coin

A small pool of muddy water

To sleep lightly

SQUAWK

SLUMBER

YUMMY

Answers on page 116

SKY-HIGH

Find all 10 things that fly.

- ☐ AIRPLANE
- ☐ HUMMINGBIRD
- ☐ HELICOPTER
- ☐ ROCKETSHIP
- ☐ DRAGONFLY
- ☐ MOSQUITO
- ☐ DRONE
- ☐ BAT
- ☐ LADYBUG
- ☐ BALLOON

```
R L D I I H E L I C O P T E R
D L A R B Q A Y B B A T S O A
A H T I E E U B I A T T D T B
T E P T S R B R H E L M S O T
D I R H U I G O U O A L R R B
R H O L A N D I M K D D O L G
A C C I S Y O Y M I U R N O E
G A K B I I I L I A U N A E N
O C E H I S O R N D O T U Q O
N O T B O Y E S G P R E K L G
F M S O L A D Y B U G O E B B
L C H M O S Q U I T O E N B A
Y B I P N A A I R P L A N E M
U O P O O I O R D B T D Y U K
U U G O M O M I B B B P S I L
```

ROADWORK AHEAD

Search for these 10 vehicles.

- ☐ DUMP TRUCK
- ☐ RACE CAR
- ☐ MOTORCYCLE
- ☐ SCHOOL BUS
- ☐ AMBULANCE
- ☐ BICYCLE
- ☐ MINIVAN
- ☐ LIMOUSINE
- ☐ SCOOTER
- ☐ JALOPY

```
I O U A E E C O K E C J
L E I Y C O M S L M O C
O O T R A M O V C C U A
R O A M M U L P I A A M
O R E T B D I Y S L L E
C C C A U U M P C N L S
M N R L L M O S O C O C
I J O B A P U S O M J H
N A M C N T S E T O L O
I L O C C R I T E T N O
V O O M E U N C R O B L
A P I R A C E C A R E B
N Y R Y V K I R I C C U
D Y U E M S C S E Y T S
E B I C Y C L E V C Y I
O B A R B I B U I L C K
L R M C S B V V Y O E M I
```

DID YOU KNOW?

An old, beat-up car is called a JALOPY.

SHINE BRIGHT

Seek out the 8 gems and crystals in this treasure trove.

- [ ] DIAMOND
- [ ] RUBY
- [ ] SAPPHIRE
- [ ] EMERALD
- [ ] Rose QUARTZ
- [ ] TOPAZ
- [ ] AMETHYST
- [ ] TURQUOISE

Search for the words in CAPITAL LETTERS!

```
L S H A S E E A M E P A U S I
Q T A I M P H Z D S R M Z T R
I U O M U A E T Q I D U A A L
E T A D R M E M E R A L D P Z
A E M R U B Y R U A E M L A M
T S E A T P Z T I A T D O R R
Q P T Y M Z E E I I U E O N P
M N H I M P T O Q I S R T Y D
D R Y T Q N I U D S Q Q T U H
S T S E T E D R M S S Z M P P
T O T I I M R P R Y N U I I T
S P D U R D Q U U A L U D E L
S A P P H I R E D E M U R R I
R Z O Q B L Y O D R I A E E R
T I N U M N T U R Q U O I S E
```

CRYSTAL QUIZ

See if you can match the gemstone to the right color.

TURQUOISE

RUBY

ROSE QUARTZ

SAPPHIRE

DIAMOND

EMERALD

AMETHYST

TOPAZ

Answers on page 117

BOW WOW

Find all 10 terr-ruff-ic dogs.

- ☐ POODLE
- ☐ TERRIER
- ☐ BOXER
- ☐ DALMATIAN
- ☐ CORGI
- ☐ COLLIE
- ☐ BULLDOG
- ☐ WHIPPET
- ☐ LABRADOR
- ☐ HUSKY

```
C O A T S P R P C O L I E A R
O L O E E O A C I X H U S K Y
K R G R L A E O I P R L D D P
B L E R O P D R R E G B A L I
D T R I Y R R G C K D O H A A
R A A E O X B I O W R X C B P
O L L R D R I U L C K E C R O
N D O M R L R M L Y O R L A O
W C L P A E I L I L L Y I D D
G H R A W T S H E P D P B O L
E L I D P R I T P Y B O E R E
G U P P E R P A U L U U G D S
G O T E P O H D N C K E P X A
R E L R T E E A R T H E A H R
L B T I O R T U S O P O T L C
```

CHIRP, CHIRP

Unscramble these 9 names of beautiful birds.

G A E L E

_ _ _ _ _

A W H K

_ _ _ _

O L A N M F I G

_ _ _ _ _ _ _ _

R O P S A R W

_ _ _ _ _ _ _

N O R B I

_ _ _ _ _

P R O T R A

_ _ _ _ _ _

F U N P F I

_ _ _ _ _ _

L B E U D I B R

_ _ _ _ _ _ _ _

W O C R

_ _ _ _

WORD BANK

- ☐ FLAMINGO
- ☐ PARROT
- ☐ BLUEBIRD
- ☐ HAWK
- ☐ PUFFIN
- ☐ EAGLE
- ☐ ROBIN
- ☐ CROW
- ☐ SPARROW

Answers on page 117

JURASSIC PLANET

Find 9 Jurassic dinosaurs and other animals of the time.

```
B B R A C H I O S A U R U S H
A L A A R L I A B D T U A L O
R G S C U S S O O I R S A O O
O C S L G R T O G L E I H I C
S B U O I S E L U O M C O C C
A T I A S P G S A P A H A S U
U L U H S A O U N H U T P S O
R U L N I G S E L O S H G A Y
U D T O N P A R O S A Y R L S
S Y U I S O U A N A U O O R I
S S S A D A R S G U R S O P S
R S C M D C U U S R U A U B O
S O I L O A S R U U S U R U U
D I P L O D O C U S L R R R U
S R U U U S I U U S S I G A O
```

- ☐ BRACHIOSAURUS
- ☐ STEGOSAURUS
- ☐ BAROSAURUS
- ☐ DIPLODOCUS
- ☐ GUANLONG
- ☐ ICHTHYOSAUR
- ☐ ALLOSAURUS
- ☐ DILOPHOSAURUS
- ☐ EMAUSAURUS

CRETACEOUS CREATURES

Spot 9 Cretaceous creatures hidden here.

- [ ] VELOCIRAPTOR
- [ ] TYRANNOSAURUS
- [ ] TROODON
- [ ] TRICERATOPS
- [ ] ANKYLOSAURUS
- [ ] SPINOSAURUS
- [ ] TALARURUS
- [ ] OVIRAPTOR
- [ ] HADROSAURUS

```
T R I C E R A T O P S A R
S T U R L U Y T U R I N S
H A D R O S A U R U S K P
T A L A R U R U S R A Y I
U S O T A T Y R S S T L N
U T I V R N S E U P R O O
T O T E I O S U U O R S S
T I V L R R O L A R C A A
O P Y O R A A D A R T U U
N R A C A A R P O R E R R
U R R I S P E O T N U U U
L R A R Y T D A T O C S S
T Y R A N N O S A U R U S
N Y E P O A I D A R I R O
R A R T T A R P P P O S R
I S O O O V S V R P A R R
S N N R A O T S L E C T R
```

Answers on page 117

THIS IS HUGE!

Find these 9 words that mean BIG.

```
U O Z E I M I W H O P P I N G M M
B G O M U M T S U P E R S I Z E D
H U Z M E B P J G G E C N G A T C
G M M D A A D U E I A G O P E M U
S E A M Z M W M G U I G R M T E
E M H A H S M B A U N A G J J H A
G R N M I M L O I M M E N S E J A
P I G E A S P T T G Z H J T S D S
A P M I I R G N D H E C G M I U H
E H H H S N N W U N P I I O N C M
N N M O E E H U N N D S H M O R G
O H H P H O G M L A R G E S O U W
R O U P T B O O O H P M R O G I L
M N S G A M A C G J R N E P R R R
O M B G E W O E M E U A R R J M P
U U G C H S B Z S B I M S M O B P
S E Z I G Z L M M E W H O I U O U
```

- ☐ LARGE
- ☐ ENORMOUS
- ☐ GIGANTIC
- ☐ MAMMOTH
- ☐ HUGE
- ☐ IMMENSE
- ☐ JUMBO
- ☐ SUPERSIZED
- ☐ WHOPPING

SHRINK It DOWN!

Find these 7 words that mean SMALL.

```
U U N L C P E I Y T P N I O S
Y I E I T E A N N C Y T R I U
Z N N L I T T L E M N E S G T
P R Y I K I T I E Z M E O D L
P C P C I T E E T D T N S K M
I R L I N E I G E P M T M A I
N M C I E E R C N N N I Y R N
T S N T G T K I I S S N G A I
S G I T T A T U I E S Y I T A
I U E M I P I T U N L I C T T
Z I N T I N N S I I S N I I U
E C M R C C E Y E E T E D A R
D I N D N I R O D I N R Y L E
I Y T N S E E O Y N C E I M E
E L O N I E N O I I Z S Y I I
```

- ☐ LITTLE
- ☐ TEENSY
- ☐ MINIATURE
- ☐ TINY
- ☐ PETITE
- ☐ PINT-SIZED
- ☐ MICRO

Answers on page 118

RECIPE FOR SUCCESS

Spell the ingredients correctly to make a tasty soup.

STEP ONE

Cook one chopped _ _ _ _ _ in a pan with some oil.

UNYON   OR   ONION

STEP TWO

Add some _ _ _ _ _ _ _ , cut into circles.

CARROTS   OR   CAROOTS

STEP THREE

Toss in some sliced _ _ _ _ _ _.

SELARY   OR   CELERY

STEP FOUR

Season with some salt and _ _ _ _ _ _.

PEPPER   OR   PEPPAR

STEP FIVE

Add some chopped _ _ _ _ _ _ _ _ _.

(ZOOKEENI)   OR   (ZUCCHINI)

STEP SIX

Pour in some _ _ _ _ _ _ _ _ _ _ stock
and simmer before serving.

(VEJETIBLE)   OR   (VEGETABLE)

STEP SEVEN

Enjoy your soup! It tastes _ _ _ _ _ _ _ _ _ _!

(DELICIOUS)   OR   (DELISHOUS)

Answers on page 118

ICE AGE BEASTS

Travel back in time to discover 8 animals from the Ice Age.

```
N R N N A V L R H I N O C E R O S
D O T T H O N O D O T M T P O V B
T M A S T O D O N O T N H P I O D
O X D E R I I Y O R A G I H E S T
O T D X H B R G L Y P T O D O N T
S O S O C I E Y A S S R O O S O H
D E O E D M R A N O O T R R R D E
L O H R N N S D V N N D S M M N O
O V R O E I D L R E I N D E E R O
V P H T N Y X T O E R O D A E E N
O X E N M A M M O T H R O N N E S
R T Y E E O A H A N H B O D E R H
```

Search the word CAPITAL LETTERS.

- ☐ MAMMOTH
- ☐ Ground SLOTH
- ☐ GLYPTODON
- ☐ REINDEER
- ☐ OXEN
- ☐ Giant BEAVER
- ☐ Woolly RHINOCEROS
- ☐ MASTODON

FOSSIL FINDS

Solve archaeological clues to complete this crossword.

DID YOU KNOW?

COPROLITE is the word for fossilized poop!

ACROSS

5. Skeletons are made from these

6. A scientist who digs for clues about ancient plants and animals

8. Something found or learned for the first time

9. Very old

DOWN

1. A scientist who digs for clues about past human life

2. A spiral-shelled fossil

3. Events of the past

4. Extinct creatures that once roamed Earth

7. The remains of a plant or animal preserved in rock or soil

8. Scooping soil in search of ancient items

WORD BANK

- [ ] ARCHAEOLOGIST
- [ ] DIGGING
- [ ] HISTORY
- [ ] BONES
- [ ] DINOSAURS
- [ ] DISCOVERY
- [ ] AMMONITE
- [ ] FOSSIL
- [ ] ANCIENT
- [ ] PALEONTOLOGIST

Answers on page 118

WORD WHIZ

Can you find all 8 wonderful words?

- ☐ NEIGHBOR
- ☐ LOYAL
- ☐ XYLOPHONE
- ☐ BAMBOOZLE
- ☐ TRICYCLE
- ☐ HEIRLOOM
- ☐ FLEECE
- ☐ ROBOT

```
Y B C O O B T H H I Y H Y M Y
L L R Y Y F L E E C E G I P I
L L O E Y A C I I M E N A N B
T M L L E Y O T R B N E P O I
E E T R I C Y C L E L I E C C
R O N R B L R L O C X Y E H O
F M Y B E N E H O E Y B Y R G
L R O N A B I O M A A L O N Z
C O G N E M Y B R C O L E L N
M B L C R I B O O O B Z Y P I
T O Y L O B G O O L O L H O H
O T X Y L O P H O N E L E A C
L O L F E I M E B Z I E H L L
I E M L Y N Y E O O L O Y A L
Y I P O O A C Z Y E R E T A H
```

WORD WHIZ QUIZ

Match each word to its definition.

BAMBOOZLE

LOYAL

ROBOT

NEIGHBOR

TRICYCLE

FLEECE

XYLOPHONE

HEIRLOOM

To trick or deceive someone

A three-wheeled vehicle similar to a bike

Someone who lives nearby

Showing constant support to someone or something

Something special handed down from one generation to another

The woolly coat of a sheep

A machine that looks or acts like a human

A musical instrument made with wooden bars

Answers on page 118

TOTAL TRANSFORMATION

Learn about metamorphosis with this cool crossword.

ACROSS

1. The early form of an insect that transforms
4. A young frog or toad
5. A silky envelope where caterpillars become moths or butterflies
6. A colorful insect with big wings

DOWN

1. All of the stages an insect goes through as it grows (two words)
2. A worm-like young form of a fly
3. An insect that looks similar to a butterfly and is active at night

WORD BANK

- [ ] BUTTERFLY
- [ ] TADPOLE
- [ ] MAGGOT
- [ ] LARVA
- [ ] COCOON
- [ ] MOTH
- [ ] LIFE CYCLE

DID YOU KNOW?
Butterflies begin life as caterpillars, and frogs hatch as tadpoles. They both undergo METAMORPHOSIS, or transformation, as they grow.

SUPER-SPEEDY ANIMAL QUIZ

Quiz yourself about some high-speed animals.

1. Which spotted cat is the fastest land animal on Earth?

- **A** Bengal
- **B** Cheetah
- **C** Leopard
- **D** Jaguar

2. How fast can a black marlin swim?

- **A** 10,000 miles per hour
- **B** 25 miles per hour
- **C** 80 miles per hour
- **D** 50 miles per hour

3. What pesky insect can zip around at 90 miles per hour?

- **A** Gnat
- **B** Hornet
- **C** Horsefly
- **D** Mosquito

4. In what countries are roadrunners found?

- **A** United States and Mexico
- **B** Australia and New Zealand
- **C** Spain and Portugal
- **D** South Africa and Mozambique

5. Kangaroos can move really fast, but they don't run. How do they get around?

- **A** Swimming
- **B** Bouncing
- **C** Rolling
- **D** Flying

Answers on page 119

ON THE FARM

Unscramble these 10 fantastic farm words.

L I G E P T

_ _ _ _ _ _

A R B N

_ _ _ _

S O H R E

_ _ _ _ _

T O R A T R C

_ _ _ _ _ _ _

A B T L S E

_ _ _ _ _ _

T O R R O S E

_ _ _ _ _ _ _

E T A C T L

_ _ _ _ _ _

M A R F R E

_ _ _ _ _ _

P E S H E

_ _ _ _ _

A T G O

_ _ _ _

WORD BANK

- ☐ BARN
- ☐ PIGLET
- ☐ SHEEP
- ☐ GOAT
- ☐ FARMER
- ☐ HORSE
- ☐ CATTLE
- ☐ TRACTOR
- ☐ ROOSTER
- ☐ STABLE

OUT IN THE DARK

Complete this crossword about animals that come out at night.

ACROSS

2. A nocturnal bird that hoots and has large eyes

4. A mammal with a long nose and tongue that eats termites and ants

6. An African island country that is home to the lemur, a nocturnal animal

8. Nocturnal creatures prefer this over sunshine

9. A stinky nocturnal mammal that is black and white

DOWN

1. Active at nighttime and sleeping during the day

3. An African big cat that hunts at night and is covered with rosette-shaped spots

5. Little bugs that twinkle in the dark

7. Colorful nocturnal lizards with big eyes and feet that stick to surfaces

WORD BANK

- [ ] GECKOS
- [ ] LEOPARD
- [ ] DARKNESS
- [ ] MADAGASCAR
- [ ] SKUNK
- [ ] OWL
- [ ] NOCTURNAL
- [ ] AARDVARK
- [ ] FIREFLIES

Answers on page 119

REACHING THE PEAK

Search for these 10 mountain ranges and regions hidden below.

Search for the words in CAPITAL LETTERS!

- ☐ ANDES
- ☐ ROCKIES
- ☐ SIERRA Nevada
- ☐ HIMALAYAS
- ☐ Black FOREST
- ☐ ATLAS Mountains
- ☐ CASCADE Range
- ☐ Great SMOKY Mountains
- ☐ DOLOMITES
- ☐ SWISS Alps

```
E H O O O C W R S S A
S K A C I L T K O I E N
A M D O L O M I T E S D
M I I C T S S E S A R E
I O S A K R O C K I E S
A T C A S M S A F M I D
S C C A S C A D E S I T
F L A I R M A S D R O F
O A A T S T O Y L O S R
R S D C L D M K M S S S
E O H I M A L A Y A S C
S I E R R A S C E I D S
T R C W I A S O E A A E
W A A C O O S W T O E E
R R D I L S E S I F S A
R I T A S I A A A S C O
O S S H O T A I H F S O
```

DID YOU KNOW?

There are two mountain ranges called SIERRA NEVADA; one is in California, and the other is in Spain. The name means "snowy mountains" in Spanish.

DOWN THE RIVER

Find these 10 famous rivers from around the world.

```
N A A I K S A A A I R A M N I
M I G I E U S E R I A P I N M
M M G E N A E Y E I I M S N I
B N S M G N I R S M I B S M S
Z B Z N D O S N U S N O A S
S E I E I E M I Y Z B Z U O I
I Z G M I L S S I E E Z R M S
Z N Y R D S E N T U Z A I S S
N E M A A U P I A A N M G E I
E I A G N N Z L S M Y B Y M P
U S I R U G D Y O S A E U E P
S O K K B Z T E K A S Z K K I
U A R S E M T Z N N N I O O M
K O N S M E N A E A Y M N N S
Z R L E R E M A D D P A S G R
```

- [ ] Rio GRANDE
- [ ] MISSISSIPPI
- [ ] AMAZON
- [ ] YUKON
- [ ] NILE
- [ ] DANUBE
- [ ] YANGTZE
- [ ] MISSOURI
- [ ] ZAMBEZI
- [ ] MEKONG

ON THE MAP

DID YOU KNOW?

Millions of years ago, all of the continents were one giant piece of land. That ancient supercontinent was called PANGAEA.

Can you label the 7 continents?

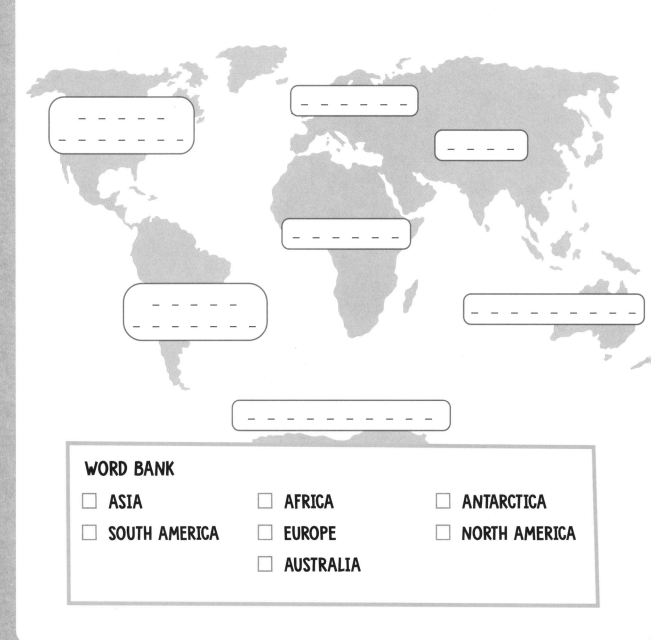

_ _ _ _ _ _ _

_ _ _ _ _ _ _

_ _ _ _ _ _

_ _ _ _ _ _

_ _ _ _ _ _

_ _ _ _ _ _ _ _

_ _ _ _ _ _ _ _ _ _ _

WORD BANK

- ☐ ASIA
- ☐ SOUTH AMERICA
- ☐ AFRICA
- ☐ EUROPE
- ☐ AUSTRALIA
- ☐ ANTARCTICA
- ☐ NORTH AMERICA

BOOM!

Find all 10 volcanic words.

```
S V A C P O R S M O O
V O L C A N O N I B U
P E R A S T V P D R B
I F A M M D R R S B E
C R I I O S A R R A A
T U F R K S B H T T N
F O S A E K L I S E A
T A A A A A A N P S M
M A A U O A S H A E R
T N A A L D T E R T M
F T G A M O A R K P K
M A G M A R R U S N L
O A S T O M P P O L K
S B K M O A E T A N A
U C R O O N V I T V T
L B D R S T T O R A S
D L R L A V A N T K H
```

DID YOU KNOW?

MAGMA is the word for liquid rock under the ground. When it breaks through the surface of the ground it is called LAVA.

MOONWALK

Astronauts have left all kinds of things on the Moon. Can you find these 9 items?

```
T H R M F L A G S R L O A
P N A S I A O F S E R F S
C E T M H R S H H A R E H
E F A H M M R F I G C A A
S R F A S E B O R M R T B
F T A R P G R O R T T H U
A R S S R E T T O S R E O
E C A M E R A P A T M R T
S C U L P T U R E S S F I
F E O O L E R I S F U U P
O U A G T S L N S F R S E
S R I F A N O T S O E R O
E S E A E C A S T O S L T
E M T R M O H G P H E T S
E R E R E U H R I M R R L
S E I S M O M E T E R S E
U O E S O A R O T I S L O
```

- ☐ FOOTPRINTS
- ☐ BOOTS
- ☐ FLAGS
- ☐ MIRRORS
- ☐ HAMMER
- ☐ FEATHER
- ☐ SCULPTURE
- ☐ CAMERA
- ☐ SEISMOMETERS

DID YOU KNOW?

SEISMOMETERS are tools that detect vibrations from earthquakes—and "moonquakes" on the Moon!

WORD MAGICIAN

Change the letters to create new words.

CHANGE ONE LETTER TO MAKE THE NEXT WORD

(T) (E) (A) (C) (H)

CLUE: To stretch out

_ E A C H

CLUE: A sweet pitted fruit

_ _ _ _ _

CLUE: Sandy spot for surf and sun

_ _ _ _ _

CLUE: A big burp

_ _ _ _ _

CHANGE TWO LETTERS TO MAKE THE NEXT WORD

(C) (R) (A) (S) (H)

CLUE: The leader of a sports team

C _ A _ H

CLUE: Another word for "dog"

_ _ _ _ _

CLUE: Something you use to bite

_ _ _ _ _

CLUE: Materials for building something

_ _ _ _ _

63

CAN YOU HEAR THAT?

Listen up! Can you find these 9 sound words?

DID YOU KNOW?

ONOMATOPOEIA is a word that imitates a sound.

- ☐ SIZZLE
- ☐ DRIP
- ☐ SPLASH
- ☐ HISS
- ☐ SCUTTLE
- ☐ BUZZ
- ☐ Pitter-PATTER
- ☐ BOOM
- ☐ POP

Search for the words in CAPITAL LETTERS!

```
S  L  P  L  S  I  U  S  L  I  S  P
T  R  P  Z  P  P  P  O  S  L  I  L
M  L  S  U  Z  O  L  A  B  U  Z  Z
O  S  O  Z  B  P  D  A  T  L  Z  T
E  T  H  L  S  D  S  P  S  T  L  E
U  P  H  L  S  R  O  P  Z  H  E  I
B  S  B  I  E  I  D  M  U  P  R  R
T  S  P  P  O  P  T  S  T  O  I  S
M  C  O  R  H  P  I  U  P  A  T  T
R  U  D  B  I  Z  U  S  S  B  H  O
B  T  Z  A  T  R  B  O  O  M  I  E
S  T  P  E  U  L  E  P  D  O  S  O
A  L  M  Z  R  E  D  E  S  O  S  I
Z  E  E  Z  O  A  E  P  T  H  B  P
I  R  E  I  D  I  Z  S  T  L  R  E
E  L  A  T  A  S  D  B  R  I  P  R
B  D  R  Z  L  E  M  T  B  O  P  L
```

POP QUIZ

Match each item to the sound it makes.

Buzz

Pitter-Patter

Hiss

Scuttle

Pop

Splash

Sizzle

Drip

Boom

Answers on page 120

ANCIENT ADVENTURE

Uncover all 12 words about ancient Egypt.

```
H S I R U E R M N R H A P I H T H
I G U A P E A P A K H O R H C S C
E H I M S S S O H O I S R O T T H
R E P S P H L C M A R N P U I R H
O O I E I A C L S U R D G H S K T
G G A S P P O E A F M A H T I E Y
L U U P I A S O Y E R M O U U N O
Y R P T H P I P I X M M I H O T X
P E S Y P Y R A M I D C O F U R P
H P A S C R I T R M P G S R Y E H
I O T A R U S R R L I G I Z A I G
C A R L A S R A C A S I T R M Y R
```

- ☐ MUMMIFY
- ☐ HIEROGLYPHIC
- ☐ KING TUT
- ☐ RAMSES
- ☐ PYRAMID
- ☐ PAPYRUS
- ☐ SPHINX
- ☐ OSIRIS
- ☐ CLEOPATRA
- ☐ PHARAOH
- ☐ GIZA
- ☐ HORUS

Answers on page 120

AWESOME!

Spot these 7 wonders of the world.

```
E P L E N C P O M T A N
C I L A T I E M O A O C
L R A Z N W U W I J P I
E R E C H J C A A M C C
M L N O A C E L H A E H
F I E L E I S L C H H I
E E L O E R R O Z A L C
H O T S A E E F M L R H
R T D S L R C C C R E E
T L H E S E L H C R D N
T H A U Z F L I C W E I
I H A M E A L N W P E T
E M U E L O I A I U M Z
F C P I C C H U H O E A
A O E Z A S O P R H R A
L E H I N R L E E R U O
R E I C P E T R A E O H
```

- ☐ Great WALL OF CHINA
- ☐ PETRA
- ☐ Christ the REDEEMER
- ☐ Machu PICCHU
- ☐ COLOSSEUM
- ☐ TAJ MAHAL
- ☐ CHICHEN ITZA

Search for the words in CAPITAL LETTERS!

WORD MAGICIAN

Change the letters to create new words.

CHANGE ONE LETTER TO MAKE THE NEXT WORD   M I L D

CLUE: Another name for your brain   M I _ D

CLUE: Blustery weather   _ _ _ _

CLUE: A magician uses this   _ _ _ _

CLUE: A body part used to hold things   _ _ _ _

CHANGE TWO LETTERS TO MAKE THE NEXT WORD   S P I C Y

CLUE: The place outside Earth   S P _ C _

CLUE: An area or region   _ _ _ _

CLUE: Something that grows   _ _ _ _

CLUE: Flavorless and dull   _ _ _ _

TOTAL OPPOSITES

Match words to their opposites to complete this crossword.

ACROSS

2. The opposite of summer
4. The opposite of awake
7. The opposite of hard

DOWN

1. The opposite of tall
2. The opposite of shout
3. The opposite of full
5. The opposite of shady
6. The opposite of under

Answers on page 121

COOL CAPITALS!

Spot the 12 U.S. capital cities hiding here.

- ☐ ANNAPOLIS
- ☐ NASHVILLE
- ☐ DENVER
- ☐ ATLANTA
- ☐ PHOENIX
- ☐ TOPEKA
- ☐ BOSTON
- ☐ OLYMPIA
- ☐ HONOLULU
- ☐ ALBANY
- ☐ JUNEAU
- ☐ MADISON

```
D J O L T O L A I P A Y
O L N I T O P E K A D U
D E N V E R L S U O L E
S A N N A P O L I S U Y
N S L B O N L O L J P T
A H O N O L U L U U H N
A U O L T S I T B N O L
I A T L A N T A E E E N
L S P A O A E O N A N O
V N U L T S N E N U I A
N M N B T H E U T S X N
O A H A M V I S N U P A
A D D N O I O O O I E B
I I E Y O L Y M P I A L
N S N T A L P E L D A S
N O L I L E P N L H A I
A N K P N O N I O Y A P
```

70

MAIN HUB

Match the country with its capital city.

 UNITED STATES

JAPAN

JORDAN

 MALAYSIA

ETHIOPIA

FIJI

 INDIA

 CANADA

PORTUGAL

ARGENTINA

 EL SALVADOR

 FRANCE

 BANGLADESH

NEW ZEALAND

KENYA

WASHINGTON, D.C.   BUENOS AIRES   KUALA LUMPUR

ADDIS ABABA   AMMAN   OTTAWA

LISBON   NEW DELHI   PARIS

DHAKA   SAN SALVADOR   WELLINGTON

TOKYO   NAIROBI   SUVA

71

Answers on page 121

WHAT DOES IT MEAN?

Can you circle the correct definition?

1. FUMBLE

A To handle something in a clumsy way

B To fall down

2. BUDGET

A A type of small yellow bird

B A plan for spending money

3. CHORTLE

A A type of turtle that sings to its young

B To laugh or chuckle

4. DEVOUR

A To eat greedily

B To make a promise

5. EMBER

A A glowing piece from a fire

B A happy memory

6. GULLIBLE

A Easily fooled or cheated

B A baby seagull

7. PENSIVE

A The lid of a pen

B Dreamy and thoughtful

8. WALLOW

A A type of pink flower

B To roll about in a lazy way

AT THE CASTLE!

Find the words among the tower of letters!

```
R R R D U N G E O N A G E T H
R G E R R N T R E A O S A T R
C C T A K O R A G L G S T L E
G R D W N E F O A E E T R R E
G E R B I G O G R A D E G L T
U N T R G T R T G A F R R U S
E E E I H A T R A R N D D Y G
T L I D T E R D E A R M T Y T
R L W G N U E G A E R O E T T
O A T E T R S T O T E A C R U
S T A R O U S Y O Y A T A R R
G I D R W O G T I N L I L T R
T O G R E L N T U R R E T N E
T N G R R O I O A R E O E A I
L N N I E O E L O R R T U N F
```

- ☐ DRAWBRIDGE
- ☐ TURRET
- ☐ MOAT
- ☐ FORTRESS
- ☐ KNIGHT
- ☐ TOWER
- ☐ DUNGEON
- ☐ CRENELLATION
- ☐ GARGOYLE

THAT'S A WRAP!

Fill in the missing letters from the words MOVIE THEATER to make movie words.

MOVIE THEATER

DI_ECTO_

ACT_NG

F_LMING

B_G SC_EEN

CU_

_ED CARP_T

B_X OFF_CE

H_LLYWO_D

SCR_PT

CRACK THE CODE

This movie fact is written in code.
Can you solve it?

20-8-5   23-15-18-4   "13-15-22-9-5"

9-19   6-18-15-13   20-8-5   20-5-18-13

"13-15-22-9-14-7   16-9-3-20-21-18-5!"

A=1	B=2	C=3	D=4	E=5	F=6
G=7	H=8	I=9	J=10	K=11	L=12
M=13	N=14	O=15	P=16	Q=17	R=18
S=19	T=20	U=21	V=22	W=23	X=24
		Y=25	Z=26		

THE _ _ _ _ "_ _ _ _ E"

_ _ _ _ _ _ THE T E _ _

"_ _ _ _ _ _ _ _ _ T _ _ E"!

Answers on page 122

GO GREEK

Find these 12 words about
ancient Greek legends.

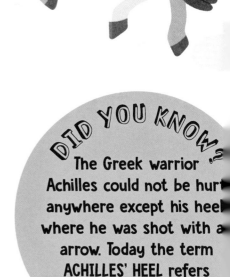

```
H O U E T R E O O H E B
S S H I I S O E E A R E
N A E T T E L E T E O E
O P R R A C H I L L E S
S U C C N S A T T S O O
A L U C S A L S Z E M H
O T L P E Z O O P E P A
E P E G A S U S L B A S
O O S C U R A T H E N A
S S S R O T T A S S D P
U S S E A P S E I O O O
E T L A E H S R M C R L
M Y T H O L O G Y I A L
E U A L I D H Z M T S O
G Z U P P O S E I D O N
N C E R B E R U S H S T
E U L U E A R S H A O E
```

DID YOU KNOW? The Greek warrior Achilles could not be hurt anywhere except his heel, where he was shot with a arrow. Today the term ACHILLES' HEEL refers to a person's "weak spot."

- ☐ HERCULES
- ☐ CERBERUS
- ☐ MYTHOLOGY
- ☐ APOLLO
- ☐ PEGASUS
- ☐ ATHENA
- ☐ ZEUS
- ☐ ARTEMIS
- ☐ PANDORA
- ☐ TITANS
- ☐ POSEIDON
- ☐ ACHILLES

THE MYTH, THE LEGEND

Uncover these 10 mythical creatures.

```
T L L G M F I L P F A E O A O T F
I A L N A W O N Y M G M L O G A R
F I I W I L E Y P E U F T E N F A
I U L F N C F A I R Y R A B O R C
B N F T M R R O H M D L W I E L C
G E L G G A D E C A H U W G T O U
N N F I D R N R R I A O R F R O N
E N O O M C F A A D L C T O O E I
F M P M O F R Y E G R R I O L D C
F M A C E N T A U R O P A T L N O
F D L E P R E C H A U N E A G H R
U N E W E R E W O L F A E L R T N
```

- ☐ UNICORN
- ☐ TROLL
- ☐ CENTAUR
- ☐ MERMAID
- ☐ DRAGON
- ☐ FAIRY
- ☐ GNOME
- ☐ LEPRECHAUN
- ☐ WEREWOLF
- ☐ BIGFOOT

PLAY BALL!

Answer these sports-themed clues for a crossword home run.

WORD BANK

- ☐ BASEBALL
- ☐ SUPERBOWL
- ☐ SOCCER
- ☐ REFEREE
- ☐ HOOP
- ☐ BEACH
- ☐ BIRDIE
- ☐ RACKET
- ☐ BOWLING
- ☐ WHISTLE

ACROSS

3. Important piece of equipment for basketball
7. A golf term that sounds like an animal name
8. This person makes sure everyone plays by the rules
9. An indoor sport with special shoes and a heavy ball

DOWN

1. Sport played with a black-and-white ball
2. This is used to hit a tennis ball
4. The game where a home run helps you win
5. It's time to stop playing when you hear this sound
6. The big football playoff, usually in February
7. Popular outdoor location for volleyball

ROCK ON!

Unscramble these musical words.

T U D E

_ _ _ _

G T A U I R

_ _ _ _ _ _

N A B D

_ _ _ _

O N I P A

_ _ _ _ _

R E N O C C T

_ _ _ _ _ _ _

S H O C U R

_ _ _ _ _ _

D A I R O

_ _ _ _ _

N O S G

_ _ _ _

WORD BANK

☐ CONCERT ☐ DUET ☐ CHORUS ☐ SONG
☐ RADIO ☐ BAND ☐ PIANO ☐ GUITAR

Answers on page 122

BACKWARD AND FORWARD

Find these 10 words that are spelled the same backward and forward.

KAYAK
ROTATOR
DEED
LEVEL
REFER
PEP
RADAR
NOON
BIB
SEES

```
D K S A O A N D S R A E K P V
A R N N O O K O R K V N A K O
S E E S O L Y A O A E R D P A
T R K F R R A R T N E A O A R
P E D A E L B V A O R S N R A
E O O K Y R I L T D T Y K E B
O N R E A A B E O R O N O S S
R A N O E R K V R K E T K A A
E A I A R I D E E D E O N K R
F E D R S S R L P E P E R N E
F R S A E O B K A A F O E Y E
E T I D R E P A N R A O E E E
N P T E A I R L K E E L D E F
K O S O T A D T E R E N A V T
A N B O A E B B R F B R D R F
```

WORD MAGICIAN

Change the letters to create new words.

CHANGE ONE LETTER TO MAKE THE NEXT WORD : T Y P E

CLUE: A sticky piece of plastic   T _ P E

CLUE: Opposite of "give"   _ _ _ _

CLUE: To create   _ _ _ _

CLUE: A tasty birthday treat   _ _ _ _

CHANGE TWO LETTERS TO MAKE THE NEXT WORD : S L O W

CLUE: Part of your forehead   _ _ O W

CLUE: The top edge of a cup   _ _ _ _

CLUE: A ray of light from the Sun   _ _ _ _

CLUE: You do this with your ears   _ _ _ _

Answers on page 123

DOWN THE RABBIT HOLE

ACROSS

2. This burrowing animal has large ears and hops to get around

7. Animals who burrow live here

9. Desert-dwelling mammal who hangs out in a "mob"

10. Underground passageways built by moles

DOWN

1. Acorn-loving burrowing rodent with big cheeks

3. To build their burrows, animals must dig a _____

4. Prairie dogs live here

5. Platypuses are found in the wild of this country only

6. This animal burrows by the river and loves to swim

8. The name of a fox's underground home

WORD BANK

- ☐ DEN
- ☐ GRASSLANDS
- ☐ RABBIT
- ☐ OTTER
- ☐ HOLE
- ☐ MEERKAT
- ☐ TUNNELS
- ☐ CHIPMUNK
- ☐ AUSTRALIA
- ☐ UNDERGROU

CORAL CHORUS

Plunge into this word search of coral reef animals.

```
R I L H F K R G R M H O O T P S A
W S A N M I R A G C R C A U A R A
A L Y O M I R R H G T I P R R O C
I E P P R D R A G O N A I T R O U
C F C O O L N T F B R F A L O E G
H O L G C I R R A Y T A C E T A A
S R O I O O R R B O P W H E F S T
O R W O R U I I L B W I O O I S O
O G N Y I N C N G E A C U C S A O
O O F I R A G S R E U N O B H R L
N S I R S A G W I O C T O P U S C
C P S U E W F I R E W O R M O R A
P S H A R K C C B O A A S I N S O
```

- ☐ CLOWNFISH
- ☐ Manta RAY
- ☐ PARROTFISH
- ☐ Sea TURTLE
- ☐ Toothy GOBY
- ☐ Reef SHARK
- ☐ Reef OCTOPUS
- ☐ Sea DRAGON
- ☐ Bearded FIREWORM

Search for the words in CAPITAL LETTERS!

SLITHERY SNAKES

Can you find all 9 sss-snakes?

```
C C T P S R A E R R G E S T S
T E V P Y R A E R N A A N C A
R E P R E I N C I S A I N O R
A I R C N G A O N R C N T P E
A N R S O T A B P A O A N P E
P O A S H E N R P I N T C E E
Y I T C A K A A T R S H R R O
T G T A O I O P R E T S P H P
H E L T R N O T A V R C V E E
O C E K A G D A T N I K S A Y
N R S S H S O A T C C P T D I
R D N T P N K D A N T O E E R
K R A C O A R K P O O H P R N
E A K C E K T K P P R R B E C
N P E I R E P H E G A R A R S
```

Search for the words in CAPITAL LETTERS!

- [ ] RATTLESNAKE
- [ ] COBRA
- [ ] PYTHON
- [ ] Boa CONSTRICTOR
- [ ] VIPER
- [ ] ANACONDA
- [ ] GARTER
- [ ] California KINGSNAKE
- [ ] COPPERHEAD

DID YOU KNOW?

OPHIDIOPHOBIA is the word for an intense fear of snakes.

Answers on page 123

LIZARD
BLIZZARD

Find 8 types of lizards.

```
O O G G S N A G N K A N E M N
H E A S N C C H A M E L E O N
R S N N D A I A C K C N U N S
E U O K O E C R E R L A D I O
G N K I C U E A E G M O R T Z
O G S G U S O T H N O N A O E
E A R U S K G O E A D U G R O
T Z H A U I E D K C A E O C N
N E R N E N C N O S N L N A C
I R S A O K K R K A G E T A N
O O N D N M O N S T E R S R U
A O A N U C M U T A T N E K O
O N M E N G R O O E G A N S H
K R S O C S N E E N L S E K L
N E A R R G G N O R K E T U E
```

- ☐ GECKO
- ☐ CHAMELEON
- ☐ Komodo DRAGON
- ☐ MONITOR Lizard
- ☐ IGUANA
- ☐ SKINK
- ☐ Gila MONSTER
- ☐ SUNGAZER

Search for the words in CAPITAL LETTERS!

Answers on page 123

BEACH DAYS

Can you complete this beach-themed crossword?

WORD BANK

- ☐ BOARDWALK
- ☐ TOWEL
- ☐ CRAB
- ☐ SURFER
- ☐ SALTWATER
- ☐ LIFEGUARD
- ☐ PACIFIC
- ☐ BUCKET
- ☐ POPSICLE
- ☐ CASTLE
- ☐ JELLYFISH
- ☐ SUNSCREEN
- ☐ VACATION

DOWN

1. A beachside structure for strolling
2. Stinging ocean dweller
4. The ocean on the West Coast of the U.S.
5. What are oceans made of?
6. Something fun to build with sand
9. The way to prevent a burn from the sun

ACROSS

3. Someone who keeps swimmers safe
4. Icy treat on a wooden stick
7. A trip away from home
8. You use this to dry off after a swim
10. Plastic tool for carrying sand and treasures
11. Someone who rides the waves on a special boar
12. Sea creature with claws

WORD MAGICIAN

Change the letters to create new words.

CHANGE ONE LETTER TO MAKE THE NEXT WORD ⋮ L I M E

CLUE: Measure this with a clock _ I M E

CLUE: The rise and fall of the ocean _ _ _ _

CLUE: Neat and clean _ _ _ _

CLUE: A word for something very small _ _ _ _

CHANGE TWO LETTERS TO MAKE THE NEXT WORD ⋮ W A V E

CLUE: To move with your feet W A _ _

CLUE: The opposite of "front" _ _ _ _

CLUE: To choose something _ _ _ _

CLUE: A place to play outside _ _ _ _

Answers on page 124

SOLAR SYSTEM SCRAMBLE

Unscramble the 8 planets in our solar system.

C E R M U R Y

_ _ _ _ _ _ _

S N E V U

_ _ _ _ _

R A T H E

_ _ _ _ _

A R M S

_ _ _ _

P R U T J I E

_ _ _ _ _ _ _

N U R A S T

_ _ _ _ _ _

S A R U N U

_ _ _ _ _ _

E N U P E N T

_ _ _ _ _ _ _

DID YOU KNOW?
Until 2006, our solar system was thought to have one more planet—Pluto. That year, scientists decided that it's actually a "dwarf planet."

SPACE QUIZ

How much do you know
about outer space?

1. What is a galaxy?

A   A type of spaceship

B   A type of rock found on the Moon

C   Astronaut food

D   A large group of stars, gas, and dust

2. What is a comet?

A   A bright space object that orbits the Sun and has a cloudy tail

B   A rocket ship made for exploring the Moon

C   A space captain

D   An ice cream from space

3. What does Martian mean?

A   A type of candy bar

B   Something from the planet Mars

C   A person who studies space

D   A type of space helmet

4. When a rocket is launched, what does that mean?

A   It's been sent into space

B   It's being used to prepare lunch

C   It's landing back on Earth

D   It's spinning in space

5. What tool helps people see space from Earth?

A   Super glasses

B   Telescope

C   Stethoscope

D   Binoculars

Answers on page 124

WORD WHIZ

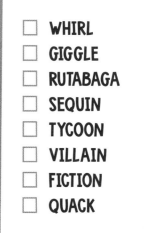

- ☐ WHIRL
- ☐ GIGGLE
- ☐ RUTABAGA
- ☐ SEQUIN
- ☐ TYCOON
- ☐ VILLAIN
- ☐ FICTION
- ☐ QUACK

Search for these 8 wacky words.

```
I S N G I G G L E T O C Q U T
V T Y C O O N A E R L O U U B
I L N T E U O T I L I A A N E
L E T I L L R T Y O N L C N A
L K S C S E Q U I N A K K N O
A A G H G Y B I T K G O O W B
I E I L T T G S N A S A E H I
N U O U O T N I N N B I G I I
I L N F N U B I B G R A I R I
I G N N I U I K Q L I R G L E
B A C O G C A S C K A I I A C
N V O I T R T T C N N O I L O
V O N Q O I I I U I N L I T W
T G U I L V R Q O W G A L N I
E O E Y I I G O T N U A C W U
```

WORD WHIZ QUIZ

Match each word to its definition.

RUTABAGA

GIGGLE

SEQUIN

QUACK

VILLAIN

FICTION

TYCOON

WHIRL

A sound made by a duck

To move in a circle

A made-up story

To laugh lightly and in a silly way

A round yellow vegetable

The evil or bad character in a story

A small shiny circle, often sewn onto clothing

A rich and powerful businessperson

Answers on page 124

HIGH COUNT

Can you spot these 8 huge number names?

```
L L O T O L T O L H T C
D O S O A D R O T G B N
O C L U L O I N O O A M
R T D N B I L L I O N T
N I O E O L L I O G O H
N L D I O O I A L O A O
D L O L I S O B L L M U
M I L L I O N I U O H S
I O T P M L N I P L N A
N N S E P T I L L I O N
N O O N I D T I G L O D
Q U A D R I L L I O N S
I I O G N E O O I T C L
N L L T C L I R O L L T
O R L I L E P A O T S L
O L M N L N N S I L I B
O O N I N L I O N L I I
```

- ☐ THOUSANDS
- ☐ TRILLION
- ☐ BILLION
- ☐ MILLION
- ☐ GOOGOL
- ☐ QUADRILLION
- ☐ SEPTILLION
- ☐ OCTILLION

SHAPE IT UP!

Can you name all of these spectacular shapes?

T _ _ _ _ _ _ _

H _ _ _ _ _ _

O _ _ _ _ _ _

R _ _ _ _ _ _ _ _ _

S _ _ _ _ _

S _ _ _ _ _ _ _ _ _

O _ _ _

S _ _ _

H _ _ _ _

Answers on page 124

SWITCH IT!

Change the first letter of each word
to match its picture.

SLOWER   _ _ _ _ _ _

LOG   _ _ _

DAMP   _ _ _ _

TEN   _ _ _

LAND   _ _ _ _

TELL   _ _ _ _

REAL   _ _ _ _

FREE   _ _ _ _

HOOK   _ _ _ _

SUPER SLEUTH

Which of these words and definitions are made-up?

LADEP
To pedal backward on a bike
○ REAL
○ FAKE

CABOOSE
A car usually at the rear of a freight train
○ REAL
○ FAKE

ASTERISK
A symbol (*) used in printing or in writing
○ REAL
○ FAKE

AMUSING
Funny and likely to make you laugh
○ REAL
○ FAKE

FENCELET
A small gate used to keep pets out of certain rooms
○ REAL
○ FAKE

PASTURE
Land where animals graze
○ REAL
○ FAKE

KHAKI
A light yellowish-brown cloth often used for pants or shorts
○ REAL
○ FAKE

MANSION
A very big, fancy house
○ REAL
○ FAKE

PLONSKIRTING
Bragging about lies
○ REAL
○ FAKE

SNOOP
To search for something in a sneaky way
○ REAL
○ FAKE

GRICKLE
A spiky plant
○ REAL
○ FAKE

Answers on page 125

SLICE
OF PARADISE

Unscramble the pizza topping words for a perfect pie.

E H E E C S

___

E O I P P P E R N

___

N O N O I

___

A P I P N E L P E

___

L O V I E S

___

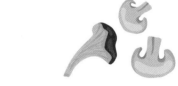

S U M O H O R M

___

L A S A M I

___

R E E P P P S

___

I SCREAM, YOU SCREAM

Scoop out these ice cream flavors.

```
E  I  V  I  E  A  O  B  A  N  R  C  C  E  L
T  P  M  A  A  O  I  R  E  R  T  L  V  I  T
R  I  N  T  N  E  A  M  A  S  Y  E  S  O  Y
T  S  P  E  R  I  C  K  C  C  I  R  S  O  C
I  T  O  T  A  M  L  T  L  R  T  S  B  B  A
K  A  E  H  R  P  A  L  O  T  E  S  R  U  C
E  C  M  I  N  T  O  E  A  R  Y  A  L  T  O
H  H  H  R  E  P  N  L  A  M  C  P  M  T  S
T  I  R  O  C  K  Y  I  I  O  K  H  T  E  R
B  O  L  H  C  S  R  E  Y  T  E  A  O  R  E
R  A  S  H  C  O  O  K  I  E  A  L  A  H  O
E  Y  T  C  O  A  L  S  V  B  C  N  O  N  O
C  Y  O  T  B  E  A  A  S  I  N  E  L  A  T
Y  R  E  P  E  C  A  N  T  Y  O  B  P  V  E
E  E  L  S  T  R  A  W  B  E  R  R  Y  I  O
```

- ☐ VANILLA
- ☐ Cookies and CREAM
- ☐ CHOCOLATE
- ☐ STRAWBERRY
- ☐ MINT Chocolate Chip
- ☐ COOKIE Dough
- ☐ Peanut BUTTER Cup
- ☐ NEAPOLITAN
- ☐ Cake BATTER
- ☐ PISTACHIO
- ☐ Butter PECAN
- ☐ ROCKY Road

Search for the words in CAPITAL LETTERS!

RHYME TIME!

Which words rhyme with these pictures?

Fill in the missing letters.

P _ _ _ _

C _ _ _

D _ _ _

T _ _ _

H _ _ _ _ _

C _ _ _ _ _

L _ _ _ _

P _ _

THE NAME OF THE GAME

It's time to find what doesn't rhyme.

1. What word does not rhyme with tough?

- **A** Rough
- **B** Puff
- **C** Stuff
- **D** Though

2. What word does not rhyme with sea?

- **A** Fee
- **B** Plea
- **C** Idea
- **D** Flea

3. What word does not rhyme with splash?

- **A** Cash
- **B** Leash
- **C** Trash
- **D** Bash

4. What word does not rhyme with sun?

- **A** Ton
- **B** Noun
- **C** Fun
- **D** Stun

5. What word does not rhyme with blue?

- **A** True
- **B** Stew
- **C** Two
- **D** Blow

Answers on page 125

CATCHING PREY

Find 8 predatory animals lurking.

- [ ] TIGER
- [ ] ORCA
- [ ] WOLF
- [ ] HYENA
- [ ] TARANTULA
- [ ] CROCODILE
- [ ] FALCON
- [ ] BEAR

```
O L A A E T O W I T U O A O U
O L E E N E A N I F L I T D E
L O L A L T A N O R I D A F E
U E R A R A R O A E F L R A E
R A O O Y T E F I L L W A L R
O A T N E A A O O O C A N C R
L B R T A R O A I T H A T O O
D O E N O I U R C C W N U N R
E L T A Y A O W L A C L L O L
W O R C R O C O D I L E A N H
A W U T R B T L C C A N R L Y
R Y T A I A O F A T A E C L E
Y F U C A G N R O O A C T A N
F L Y E D E E N C R H B I T A
R A C H A L N R E A L A L W Y
```

WORD MAGICIAN

Change the letters to create new words.

CHANGE ONE LETTER TO MAKE THE NEXT WORD

T R Y

CLUE: What you do when you're sad   _ R Y

CLUE: The opposite of "wet"   _ _ _

CLUE: The opposite of "night"   _ _ _

CLUE: You might see bales of this on farms   _ _ _

CHANGE TWO LETTERS TO MAKE THE NEXT WORD

S E A T

CLUE: What you stand on   _ E _ T

CLUE: To be afraid of something   _ _ _ _

CLUE: The number after "three"   _ _ _ _

CLUE: A very high volume   _ _ _ _

Answers on page 126

I FEEL HAPPY!

YAY! Find these 8 joyful words.

```
G L A D L B C H E E R F U L J
L L B L I S S F U L E D Y U I
L U I O D Y D L E L H A P P Y
I A D U C E S F C R L A S O E
B L D D O E X C I T E D R S A
E O T I R G G I D D Y R O A P
X G P Y I R B E R L F E L U H
R L L Y Y I H T L T F A B X E
L M H H E U L L L E F H L A G
L L E X F F H E M Y P J E E E
L O S R Y I A R L R C O D Y L
L T A B R G F E E D D L L Y D
A H S A U Y I U L Y I L Y Y S
D T O A H S E E E B I Y X E L
G R L S I O T G P F Y S L H T
```

- [ ] HAPPY
- [ ] CHEERFUL
- [ ] JOLLY
- [ ] GIDDY
- [ ] GLAD
- [ ] EXCITED
- [ ] MERRY
- [ ] BLISSFUL

DID YOU KNOW?

ECSTATIC is another joyful word. It means very, very happy!

SEEING RED

Grrr! Find these 10 angry words.

```
I D I D I M R D I G I E M D E
E U G B G G S N E D A R N I D
A N G U U A U S E M G A A Y E
N B B I A G E T I E O E S S U
A G A O G F O E E I O O O N
A N R G I O U A N O O S N D O
U B S E D L F M C R O S S O N
D I G O D F I I I G A D B O N
F E U N I G N N D N G G M A S
U G U D U N I G G R G T E A D
R F A I C M R O O C O L U D D
I O R R G S K R A T R O N R A
O U T R A G E D M S E E E U I
U R A E N E D E E D G A E E L
S E I I N G A N N O Y E D F O
```

- ☐ ENRAGED
- ☐ STEAMING
- ☐ FURIOUS
- ☐ MAD
- ☐ FUMING
- ☐ BOILING
- ☐ CROSS
- ☐ OUTRAGED
- ☐ ANNOYED
- ☐ IRKED

Answers on page 126

MY GANG

Find these 11 names
of animal groups.

DID YOU KNOW?

Names for groups
of things are
called COLLECTIVE
NOUNS.

- ☐ SWARM
- ☐ COLONY
- ☐ ARMY
- ☐ PACK
- ☐ SCHOOL
- ☐ SMACK
- ☐ PRIDE
- ☐ PARLIAMENT
- ☐ SHIVER
- ☐ POD
- ☐ PARADE

```
M O D R W S W A R M O C
R O P C M C A S C A D C
A C S C H O O L I P I O
P S N P Y L I D P P E Y
A R M Y R O P A R A D E
R S I A E N S R A R P R
A A I D C Y P O D L A A
H A A O E K R K T I K R
O P A R P C M H A A A K
I O P M O A R A O M L P
R M E R E S S K A E L A
V E D A M S E P Y N N M
R W H R Y H E A V T E P
H E M M C I O C S A O O
R L A A S V O K C K K D
N R C A R E P S P E P R
H T P P M R Y C I P O E
```

GROUP EFFORT

Match these animals to their group name.

SWARM

COLONY

ARMY

PACK

SCHOOL

SMACK

PRIDE

PARLIAMENT

SHIVER

POD

PARADE

Elephants

Lions

Bees

Fish

Whales

Ants

Wolves

Jellyfish

Owls

Sharks

Frogs

Answers on page 126

OLYMPIC GOLD!

Spot the Olympic sports.

```
M M I G H T S A R E T M G S A
W N N Y Y T A K R E L E K H N
S H S W I M M I N G E C A T A
L C J O A T N T E N N I S B A
O N M L C Y M A J N H R A S A
G R T A L C S A S U A A E S M
H R N R C M E S K T D D R T G
T R N C O Y K R O I I O T E N
S G A H N R A G U K E C A N I
D S C E S A R A R I B T S W K
R S G R L M A S K A T I N G I
G A O Y I R T Y I E S A S R A
M R B A S K E T B A L L O M K
M S A E T M M A R A T H O N E
I I N R H W M M S N S S I I Y
```

- ☐ GYMNASTICS
- ☐ SWIMMING
- ☐ MARATHON
- ☐ JUDO
- ☐ SOCCER
- ☐ BASKETBALL
- ☐ ARCHERY
- ☐ KARATE
- ☐ TENNIS
- ☐ SKATING

WELCOME TO THE MUSEUM!

Can you find the items on display?

```
L E G W L A L R E A O W I N P
L O H E A I M A P O E N P L U
T A E T R U G N L E C Y I T S
G E P L I N L W L T E T N P O
C O S M R D E I A S P S A S C
L P L U O N S E K E D L N M A
K A O D E M J C L U T O R A N
P I U S A R C O P H A G U S T
G N A K L A T U W O I S R K W
I T Y E G I Y O S S D M N O U
P I L L S C U L P T U R E E
G N T E I F W J A O W G O C U
K G L T L T T J E W E L R Y H
S P A O E D G W E A P O N H T
I A L N C F O S S I L D S A F
```

☐ SARCOPHAGUS	☐ GOLD	☐ MAP
☐ MASK	☐ PAINTING	☐ FOSSIL
☐ SKELETON	☐ SCULPTURE	☐ WEAPON
☐ JEWELRY		

DID YOU KNOW?

A SARCOPHAGUS is a stone coffin.

Answers on page 127

FIND THE ANIMAL

Each word below can be changed into the name of an animal by changing the last letter. Can you figure them out?

SLUM ــ ــ ــ ــ

BAM ــ ــ ــ

HIPPY ــ ــ ــ ــ ــ

GOAL ــ ــ ــ ــ

SHARP ── ── ── ── ──

PIN ── ── ──

SHEET ── ── ── ── ──

YAP ── ── ──

WORD ── ── ── ──

NEWS ── ── ── ──

BIRTHDAY PARTY!

You're invited to search for these 12 birthday words.

```
L A R P L A L L D S T A I A P G P
B N S N E N R Y S R K O N A C O P
N T T V H C A K E E O B V E E O R
Y P R S N D M E L P N A I Y L D E
E E E P C E R M N I T L T V E Y S
P C A N D L E S O S L L A L B I E
P O M R E A A O R C G O T O R T N
A R E H H A T L R A K O I O A S T
R T R P A H E I N L Y N O L T O S
T O S N R P A M A N G S N N I T A
Y E E S R A P T S E O C E A O G A
L C R E A M Y Y N E L R D S N Y L
```

Search for the words in CAPITAL LETTERS!

- ☐ PRESENTS
- ☐ PARTY Games
- ☐ GOODY Bag
- ☐ CANDLES
- ☐ BALLOONS
- ☐ HAPPY Birthday
- ☐ CAKE
- ☐ Party HAT
- ☐ STREAMERS
- ☐ CELEBRATION
- ☐ Ice CREAM
- ☐ INVITATION

Answers on page 127

ENGINEER THAT!

Construct this crossword by solving these clues.

Answers on page 127

ACROSS

3. Tool used for driving nails
5. Large machine used to dig into the ground and remove soil
6. Item that protects your head (two words)
7. Vehicle for moving bulky materials (two words)
8. Cart with one wheel used to carry and move heavy loads
10. Tool that makes holes

DOWN

1. Structure that joins one piece of land to another
2. Material that makes concrete
4. Very loud rock-drilling equipment
9. Place where construction happens

WORD BANK

☐ WORKSITE
☐ DUMP TRUCK
☐ EXCAVATOR
☐ JACKHAMMER
☐ WHEELBARROW
☐ HARD HAT
☐ DRILL
☐ CEMENT
☐ HAMMER
☐ BRIDGE

CAREER DAY

What might you be when you grow up?
Add the vowels to complete these job names.

A E I O U

N _ RS _

F _ R _ F _ GHT _ R

F _ RM _ R

D _ R _ CT _ R

_ RT _ ST

SC _ _ NT _ ST

D _ S _ GN _ R

T _ _ CH _ R

PR _ S _ D _ NT

WR _ T _ R

B _ _ LD _ R

CH _ F

Answers on page 127

ANSWERS

page 8 — Into the Rainforest

```
L L L A L P I A O L A G E L L
B S F G R S A N A R P P R A I
R O I R B F H R A N R O A B D
Y N M O I U L H R A G O G R O
A L T F L A D L L O N T D O O
G I B B O N H L E O T O B P I
U U A R D G I S U M O R F L C
T E L R A R O L O J U F U A C
G O R I L L A O U A C R R O A
Y R A A A O G T F G A A E O O
O O O U A A C H L U N G I R G
A L G O A O G A N A C O N D A
P E A A T T F R H R T L A N I
H S L B U T T E R F L Y O R L
P A L S O C O A O A B O M A O
```

page 9 — Desert Discoveries

```
L E O T A R M R S E T O
R T P M E E E U A E E I
A M E I R N E A N M H D
L E K A O S R N D O C D
H A R E L E K I C D N K
E Y N S R A A H A A C A
O O E C E C T Y T E R R
C S I O I E O A S K J M
E I Y R A S A C E W R A
E D A P T A I O A S E D
M E E I T E D Y D M I I
R W E O N A O O O R E L
R I E N A N A T E A E L
I N D A E E T E D R E O
N D P O J E R B O A R C
I E O H S A R D E E R D
D R R O A D R U N N E R
```

page 10 — Wild Ocean

N G I E P N U: Penguin

L O N I D P H: Dolphin

A H E S E O R S: Seahorse

B C R A: Crab

Q I D U S: Squid

page 11 — Word Magician

MAPS – MOPS – HOPS – POPS – PUPS

LANE – TUNE – DONE – NINE – KIND

page 12 — Little Friends

ACROSS	DOWN
4. Foal	1. Puppy
5. Piglet	2. Tadpole
7. Joey	3. Kitten
8. Snakelet	6. Duckling
9. Cygnet	9. Calf

page 13 — Animal Expert

1. Cygnet

2. Piglet

3. Snakelet

4. Duckling

5. Joey

page 14 — Towering Trees

```
O L L R R G Y R D C Y W L
R O G C H E R R Y E M O O
S R T D O O M O R L L W O
D S Y C A M O R E W O I M
A D A A R R C D M A E L R
R E V E R G R E E N O L E
E W O C H E S T N U T O N
E O A E O E V N W I O W L
L D K E M A P L E W O T V
Y O L O H R N O R Y L M M
R P V L G E L K G E O P A
G E W Y K D E N R A V E G
L D D S R W R L E G M N N
A O D H N O A K R E E M O
O D H W D O G W O O D L L
W C I E T D K O G L E M I
R H W W G A D R Y D N G A
```

page 15 — Fabulous Flowers

```
D F U W T S F D R U E O T U O O L
R L E H R L T U V I O L E T D C C
D C Y K O L N O O F O R H I A H E
S W D E D L A V T E D V O R F E Y
S E L S U N F L O W E R N S F R O
U C R F H S O H B P R K E I O R O
L T A T R F R O Y C E O Y I D Y U
E R D D U W B O L H E R S R I B M
E U A P E L I F F E R S U E L L T
R V I D O E I T U E U L C R L O T
N O S F E K C P R D E E K B P S Y
H A Y M E W C H O Y R I L O O S S
O S I E I I I D L U K A E R T O I
D P E R I W I N K L E S L T I M T
B U T T E R C U P O T I S E M T M
U S E B A Y A I E U S E M L B D E
```

page 16 — Word Whiz

```
Y S L P O S D O R H R O E E R O
Q B D I L N O L I U A I T T A P
L B N I O O A L Q L V U B O O L
N A D N D L L S B L S V E N B I
Y U B T O D I U N A Q O B I R E
D A L R N B N P B B U O L P A O
E B D A A T R E E A A O O U B O
P U O I Y D I R D L B R A V R A
O U T Q A A O N S O B O D U O F
M A E B B L I O O L L U N O O
N E B N E B A V D O E L Q H E A
I L D U O O O A N L U U O L N E
V N D A R B L U N D E R F P E I
O D Y N D E B O I I S U O O L Y
R I N F I N I T Y B B D S L E L
E O M E U T O A R N L B O D I R
```

page 17 — Word Whiz Quiz

HULLABALOO: A loud, continued noise or mixture of noises

OMNIVORE: An animal that eats both plants and meat

LABRADOODLE: A dog that is a cross between a Labrador retriever and a poodle

DOLLOP: A spoonful of something soft or mushy

SUPERNOVA: An exploding star

BLUNDER: A silly mistake

INFINITY: An unlimited space, amount, or period of time

SQUABBLE: A fight over something that is not important

page 18 — Come One, Come All!

ACROSS	DOWN
2. Magician	1. Unicycle
4. Ticket	3. Cotton Candy
6. Juggling	5. Tightrope
9. Ringmaster	7. Big Top
10. Popcorn	8. Grandstand
12. Clowns	11. Net

page 19 — Word Magician

SOUP - SOAP - SOAR - SOUR - HOUR

BOOK - POOL - PULL - CALL - CAVE

page 20 — Time for Action!

```
T A S T E S A E E R U
S S R A S T I P T O E S
J U G G L E E L T E H I
E C S S E H U C L L E S
T T R W H I S T L E A W
J G L U W T L S H D R U
C S U L D I S C U S S O
A A R L W U R G E I E S
S U L H A R E L E E E O
E P S C L B S A G W R E
E U H S U E W E T E U S
E S P T T L T C E L P G
P T E R R L A H W I T G
W U R E S O H T A C H W
L A H T C W T P E U D P
C J S C O H A T S A T R
H S E H C E A O S U S S
```

page 21 — Quickly, Slowly

```
U S T E E S S Y Y E S A E L Y L
L A C L E A F U O I L C Y E I E
Y L Y E F Y L O Y N E S E F O S
R S E B E E F O O E O E H L I I
S I I B R O F E R L P C I A E L
V P E C M A P E E I I P E P T E
E Q E I R I V E R Q L S S P I N
O U S P U E C E S I Y O H I A T
E I P P R A E L L E L R T L L L
N E I Y S I M P L Y N L P Y Y Y
L T I Y R F L F I E R C E L Y L
I L F E Y L E Y E L L R O I Y B
N Y N B N T Y A P H Y Y E Y L A
L Y Y F O R T U N A T E L Y L L
L I U Y N E A E L I Y B L F Y L
```

page 22 — It's a Rainbow!

```
Y B V I O L E T I L O I N E E
N L Y Y N E R G R R E E O T L
B L U E E D E E O D B A R B E
G R L O L O I Y I L E R U W R
E E Y E E L G G L I Y T E E E
W V L L A N O N O R L E R E D
A D O E D G L W W L W R E O G
O B R U E T E L I R E I I I Y
O U A O O L E Y E N U R O E E
G E N L L N L W R B I N R E D
E R G E R O R A G L O E L L O
E I E R N V O D T E R E N R A
R I N E E I V I E E O R E R O
L N T E B E O O G A G T R L O
U N O O E L N N D B U L N U L
```

page 23 — Wild Weather

BLIZZARD	SNOW
CLOUDY	LIGHTNING
SLEET	RAIN
HEATWAVE	THUNDER
HAIL	TORNADO

page 24 — Star Chart

```
R O R O D D G D E N I R P V E
U S D A B I I G R M D B A M E
I B U Y N A V B R A D A A R D
D R N I T S P B D R R R U A I
O N G H N A G R U N I R E B I
R I R Y P R U E R U E I M I R
N E R D T R A R I E S A A G E
R A V R T N A R U I R R H D R
S U I A R S D A R S R G D I P
I N R I R T A E P A S E I P I
P S G S S N N A H N G M D P N
M O O R I O N B E U E I O E G
M G A N D R O M E D A N G R M
T R T A V R A G O I A I E I V
D N A R N I P R N I I A N S G
```

page 25 — Secret Stellar Codes

SAG GNINRUB FO EDAM ERA SRATS
Stars are made of burning gas

SEIXALAG DELLAC SPUORG NI DNUOF
ERA SRATS
**Stars are found in groups
called galaxies**

EULB ERA SRATS TSETTOH EHT
The hottest stars are blue

YAW YKLIM EHT DELLAC SI YXALAG RUO
Our galaxy is called the Milky Way

pages 26–27 — Super Sleuth

1. A	7. A
2. A	8. B
3. A	9. B
4. B	10. A
5. A	11. B
6. A	

page 28 — Busy Body

```
K A L A F O C L O T N G E
E B E A N A T T O O B A O
O D F L C K E U B N L I T
E T E B O A L A B G O N W
E E N E E T B E O U T H I
F N K N A E O A G E R I B
L F A B R L W E C O N G E
F L F K L F F A N K E R L
F O O T O O A R K A E L O
A R L K B B K H O A I L F
L F O R E H E A D T N L O
L E T T A O T E E E E T N
O L K E E T A L A D N B L
A L L N T O O L A B R G A
I E E B I A L A O N O N K
A L A E A E W T E E A L F
A O T B N E L U U W W O E
```

page 29 — Word Magician

MOON – MOOS – MOOD – FOOD – GOOD

SEED – SAND – POND – CONE – MANE

page 30 — Sensational!

```
W E C S H C Y C G P Y I C S S
H I N I R Y M H S O L P T P G
S C U Y S T U E O O S H O C P
P S Y S H H S W E P C G O I O
S C R A T C H Y Y H C Y Y Y I
H P M T T L Y H L S R Y H I N
Y C I M C Y M I C O O R Y Y T
O M I K N T M S H G O H P C Y
Y S D U Y U C O T G H S C U Y
G S C K L S R C Y Y Y D D H
Y M N S Y P I C G S C S S D M
T O Y C U I S L I M Y D Y L P
C O Y S S M P M S I U I L Y I
S T Y T A Y Y Y E H O P O D U
I H I D W M H Y K T I H T S P
```

page 31 — Stuck Together

```
A P H M R R R W L R S E
D I H S Y R U A P H E S
R L C A E I R R W W Y E A
S O S T L L I R W A C G
S W I A S A H Y A I R U
W C R O S S W A L K D L
E A A A B Y O R K E L L
A S T R A C E T R A C K
T E D Y R E H G K R U S
S G S A N G S B C A R K
H A R W Y S E D S A L A
I L A I A T O A W R I A
R E E P R K I L T I B Y
T E W L D W D M K A C S
D O L L H O U S E L O H
H P D I S H W A S H E R
```

page 32 — Fruit Bowl

ANBAAN: Banana
ERAP: Pear
HERCRY: Cherry
WIIK: Kiwi
GANMO: Mango
CAPEH: Peach
PLEPA: Apple
GPRAE: Grape
ALETENWORM: Watermelon
RSWATERBYR: Strawberry

page 33 — Bake Sale

```
T I R I E I O O B K R T
C R R S K K N S T C B I
G N P R B R O W N I E S
E O T L R R S S E T E E
S P R I N K L E S B S K
F C T S U G W I E A N P
C R F T H E O K R T D K
A A R O E O P A S T R Y
A G I N G E R B R E A D
O D M O B K C T A R U O
O U U U T I U A C R I U
A N F A A O P E O A A G
E L F B I D C N F G K H
C N I I O D A D E G T E
E A N C O O K I E R Y R
I Y G I O R E O P U A A
R G R E P T I K O T R B
```

page 34 — In-Tents!

ACROSS
2. Smores
4. Stargaze
5. Campfire
8. Sleeping bag
9. Hike

DOWN
1. Ghost stories
3. Backpack
6. Flashlight
7. Tents

page 35 — Campfire Quiz

1. B 2. C 3. D 4. A

page 36 — Word Whiz

```
B U Z A U D Y U I Q Z Y A L B
L L A R A D P U D D L E V E V
K Z M R E E L D U L U N O Q P
E A R K P A R K A V U L C R S
S Q U A W K N L R S A U A M N
M U C M M E E I A E K D B M S
P E U A A D Y E C U L E U N L
R E L E I S N D S K D K L V W
A D U A B C L N U R E B A E P
N R B B K Q T U M T Y L R D M
D Y U A L L Z U M S E U Y V A
O A C Z D A N L Z B Z C M D R
M B K V U K U L E L E L U M A
L R P Y C C A R S N P R R U Y
U U E O D U L U T E D A A U M
```

page 37 — Word Whiz Quiz

ZEST: An exciting quality
YUMMY: Great-tasting
RANDOM: Without a clear pattern
PARKA: A warm, windproof winter coat
SQUAWK: A short, harsh cry often made by birds
VOCABULARY: A collection of words and their meanings
UKULELE: A small instrument similar to a guitar
NICKEL: A five-cent coin
PUDDLE: A small pool of muddy water
SLUMBER: To sleep lightly

page 38 — Sky-High

```
R L D I I H E L I C O P T E R
D L A R B Q A Y B B A T S O A
A H T I E E U B I A T D T D T B
T E P T S R B R H E L M S O T
D I R H U I G O U O A L R R B
R H O L A N D I M K D D O L G
A C C I S Y O Y M I U R N O E
G A K B I I I L A U N A E N
O C E H I S O R N D O T U Q O
N O T B O Y E S G P R E K L G
F M S O L A D Y B U G O E B B
L C H M O S Q U I T O E N B A
Y B I P N A A I R P L A N E M
U O P O O I O R D B T D Y U K
U U G O M O M I B B B P S I L
```

page 39 — Roadwork Ahead

```
I O U A E E C O K E C J
L E I Y C O M S L M O C
O O T R A M O V C C U A
R O A M M U L P I A A M
O R E T B D I Y S L L E
C C C A U U M P C N L S
M N R L L M O S O C O C
I J O B A P U S O M J H
N A M C N T S E T O L O
I L O C C R I T E T N O
V O O M E U N C R O B L
A P I R A C E C A R E B
N Y R Y V K I R I C C U
D Y U E M S C S E Y T S
E B I C Y C L E V C Y I
O B A R B I B U I L C K
L R M C S B V V Y O E M I
```

page 40 — Shine Bright

```
L S H A S E E A M E P A U S I
Q T A I M P H Z D S R M Z T R
I U O M U A E T Q I D U A A L
E T A D R M E M E R A L D P Z
A E M R U B Y R U A E M L A M
T S E A T P Z T I A T D O R R
Q P T Y M Z E E I I U E O N P
M N H I M P T O Q I S R T Y D
D R Y T Q N I U D S Q Q T U H
S T S E T E D R M S S Z M P P
T O T I I M R P R Y N U I I T
S P D U R D Q U U A L U D E L
S A P P H I R E D E M U R R I
R Z O Q B L Y O D R I A E E R
T I N U M N T U R Q U O I S E
```

116

page 41 — Crystal Quiz

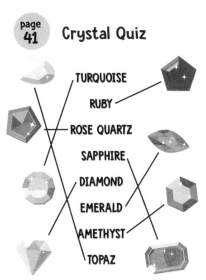

TURQUOISE
RUBY
ROSE QUARTZ
SAPPHIRE
DIAMOND
EMERALD
AMETHYST
TOPAZ

page 42 — Bow Wow

```
C O A T S P R P C O L I E A R
O L O E E O A C I X H U S K Y
K R G R L A E O I P R L D D P
B L E R O P D R R E G B A L I
D T R I Y R R G C K D O H A A
R A A E O X B I O W R X C B P
O L L R D R I U L C K E C R O
N D O M R L R M L Y O R L A O
W C L P A E I L I L Y I D D D
G H R A W T S H E P D P B O L
E L I D P R I T P Y B O E R E
G U P P E R P A U L U U G D S
G O T E P O H D N C K E P X A
R E L R T E E A R T H E A H R
L B T I O R T U S O P O T L C
```

page 43 — Chirp, Chirp

GAELE: Eagle
AWHK: Hawk
OLANMFIG: Flamingo
ROPSARW: Sparrow
NORBI: Robin
PROTRA: Parrot
FUNPFI: Puffin
LBEUDIBR: Bluebird
WOCR: Crow

page 44 — Jurassic Planet

```
B B R A C H I O S A U R U S H
A L A A R L I A B D T U A L O
R G S C U S S O O I R S A O O
O C S L G R T O G L E I H I C
S B U O I S E L U O M C O C C
A T I A S P G S A P A H A S U
R U L N I G S E L O S H G A Y
U D T O N P A R O S A Y R L S
S Y U I S Q U A N A U O O R I
S S S A D A R S G U R S O P S
R S C M D C U U S R U A U B O
S O I L O A S R U U S U R U U
D I P L O D O C U S L R R R U
S R U U U S I U U S S I G A O
```

page 45 — Cretaceous Creatures

```
T R I C E R A T O P S A R
S T U R L U Y T U R I N S
H A D R O S A U R U S K P
T A L A R U R U S R A Y I
U S O T A T Y R S S T L N
U T I V R N S E U P R O O
T O T E I O S U U O R S S
T I V L R R O L A R C A A
O P Y O R A A D A R T U U
N R A C A A R P O R E R R
U R R I S P E O T N U U U
L R A R Y T D A T O C S S
T Y R A N N O S A U R U S
N Y E P O A I D A R I R O
R A R T T A R P P P O S R
I S O O O V S V R P A R R
S N N R A O T S L E C T R
```

page 46 — This Is Huge!

```
U O Z E I M I W H O P P I N G M M
B G O M U M T S U P E R S I Z E D
H U Z M E B P J G G E C N G A T C
G M M D A A D U E I A G O P E M U
S E A M Z M W M G U G I G R M T E
E M H A H S M B A U N A G J J H A
G R N M I M L O I M M E N S E J A
P I G E A S P T T G Z H J T S D S
A P M I I R G N D H E C G M I U H
E H H H S N N W U N P I I O N C C
N N M O E E H U N N D S H M O R G
O H H P H O G M L A R G E S O U W
R O U P T B O O O H P M R O G I L
M N S G A M A C G J R N E P R R R
O M B G E W O E M E U A R R J M P
U U G C H S B Z S B I M S M O B P
S E Z I G Z L M M E W H O I U O U
```

Shrink It Down!

```
U U N L C P E I Y T P N I O S
Y I E I T E A N N C Y T R I U
Z N N L I T T L E M N E S G T
P R Y I K I T I E Z M E O D L
P C P C I T E E T D T N S K M
I R L I N E I G E P M T M A I
N M C I E E R C N N N I Y R N
T S N T G T K I I S S N G A I
S G I T T A T U I E S Y I T A
I U E M I P I T U N L I C T T
Z I N T I N N S I I S N I I U
E C M R C C E Y E E T E D A R
D I N D N I R O D I N R Y L E
I Y T N S E E O Y N C E I M E
E L O N I E N O I I Z S Y I I
```

Recipe for Success

STEP ONE: onion
STEP TWO: carrots
STEP THREE: celery
STEP FOUR: pepper
STEP FIVE: zucchini
STEP SIX: vegetable
STEP SEVEN: delicious

Ice Age Beasts

```
N R N N A V L R H I N O C E R O S
D O T T H O N O D O T M T P O V B
T M A S T O D O N O T N H P I O D
O X D E R I I Y O R A G I H E S T
O T D X H B R G L Y P T O D O N T
S O S O C E Y A S S R O O S O H
D E O E D M R A N O O T R R R D E
L O H R N N S D V N N D S M M N O
O V R O E I D L R E I N D E E R O
V P H T N Y X T O E R O D A E E N
O X E N M A M M O T H R O N N E S
R T Y E E O A H A N H B O D E R H
```

Fossil Finds

ACROSS
5. Bones
6. Paleontologist
8. Discovery
9. Ancient

DOWN
1. Archaeologist
2. Ammonite
3. History
4. Dinosaurs
7. Fossil
8. Digging

Word Whiz

```
Y B C O O B T H H I Y H Y M Y
L L R Y Y F L E E C E G I P I
L L O E Y A C I I M E N A N B
T M L L E Y O T R B N E P O I
E E T R I C Y C L E L I E C C
R O N R B L R L O C X Y E H O
F M Y B E N E H O E Y B Y R G
L R O N A B I O M A A L O N Z
C O G N E M Y B R C O L E L N
M B L C R I B O O O B Z Y P I
T O Y L O B G O O L O L H O H
O T X Y L O P H O N E L E A C
L O L F E I M E B Z I E H L L
I E M L Y N Y E O O L O Y A L
Y I P O O A C Z Y E R E T A H
```

Word Whiz Quiz

BAMBOOZLE: To trick or deceive someone
TRICYCLE: A three-wheeled vehicle similar to a bike
NEIGHBOR: Someone who lives nearby
LOYAL: Showing constant support to someone or something
HEIRLOOM: Something special handed down from one generation to another
FLEECE: The woolly coat of a sheep
ROBOT: A machine that looks or acts like a human
XYLOPHONE: A musical instrument made with wooden bars

page 54 — Total Transformation

ACROSS
1. Larva
4. Tadpole
5. Cocoon
6. Butterfly

DOWN
1. Life cycle
2. Maggot
3. Moth

page 55 — Super-Speedy Animal Quiz

1. B
2. C
3. A
4. A
5. B

page 56 — On the Farm

L I G E P T: Piglet
A R B N: Barn
S O H R E: Horse
T O R A T R C: Tractor
A B T L S E: Stable
T O R R O S E: Rooster
E T A C T L: Cattle
M A R F R E: Farmer
P E S H E: Sheep
A T G O: Goat

page 57 — Out in the Dark

ACROSS
2. Owl
4. Aardvark
6. Madagascar
8. Darkness
9. Skunk

DOWN
1. Nocturnal
3. Leopard
5. Fireflies
7. Geckos

page 58 — Reaching the Peak

```
E H O O O C W R S S S A
S K A C I L T K O I E N
A M D O L O M I T E S D
M I I C T S S E S A R E
I O S A K R O C K I E S
A T C A S M S A F M I D
S C C A S C A D E S I T
F L A I R M A S D R O F
O A A T S T O Y L O S R
R S D C L D M K M S S S
E O H I M A L A Y A S C
S I E R R A S C E I D S
T R C W I A S O E A A E
W A A C O O S W T O E E
R R D I L S E S I F S A
R I T A S I A A A S C O
O S S H O T A I H F S O
```

page 59 — Down the River

```
N A A I K S A A A I R A M N I
M I G I E U S E R I A P I N M
M M G E N A E Y E I I M S N I
B N S M G N I R S M I B S M S
Z B Z N D O S N U N S N O A S
S E I E I E M I Y Z B Z U O I
I Z G M I L S S I E E Z R M S
Z N Y R O S E N T U Z A I S S
N E M A A U P I A A N M G E I
E I A G N N Z L S M Y B Y M P
U S I R U G D Y O S A E U E P
S O K K B Z T E K A S Z K K I
U A R S E M T Z N N N I O O M
K O N S M E N A E A Y M N N S
Z R L E R E M A D D P A S G R
```

page 60 — On the Map

page 61 — Boom!

```
S V A C P O R S M O O
V O L C A N O N I B U
P E R A S T V P D R B
I F A M M D R R S B E
C R I I O S A R R A A
T U F R K S B H T T N
F O S A E K L I S E A
T A A A A A A N P S M
M A A U O A S H A E R
T N A A L D T E R T M
F T G A M O A R K P K
M A G M A R R U S N L
O A S T O M P P O L K
S B K M O A E T A N A
U C R O O N V I T V T
L B D R S T T O R A S
D L R L A V A N T K H
```

page 62 — Moonwalk

```
T H R M F L A G S R L O A
P N A S I A O F S E R F S
C E T M H R S H H A R E H
E F A H M M R F I G C A B
S R F A S E B O R M R T A
F T A R P G R O R T T H U
A R S S R E T T O S R E O
E C A M E R A P A T M R T
S C U L P T U R E S S F I
F E O O L E R I S F U U P
O U A G T S L N S F R S E
S R I F A N O T S O E R O
E S E A E C A S T O S L T
E M T R M O H G P H E T S
E R E R E U H R I M R R L
S E I S M O M E T E R S E
U O E S O A R O T I S L O
```

page 63 — Word Magician

TEACH – REACH – PEACH – BEACH – BELCH

CRASH – COACH – POOCH – TOOTH – TOOLS

page 64 — Can You Hear That?

```
S L P L S I U S L I S P
T R P Z P P P O S L I L
M L S U Z O L A B U Z Z
O S O Z B P D A T L Z T
E T H L S D S P S T L E
U P H L S R O P Z H E I
B S B I E I D M U P R R
T S P P O P T S T O I S
M C O R H P I U P A T T
R U D B I Z U S S B H O
B T Z A T R B O O M I E
S T P E U L E P D O S O
A L M Z R E D E S O S I
Z E E Z O A E P T H B P
I R E I D I Z S T L R E
E L A T A S D B R I P R
B D R Z L E M T B O P L
```

page 65 — Pop Quiz

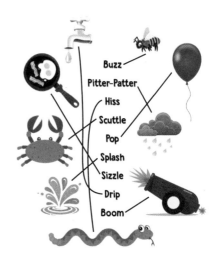

Buzz
Pitter-Patter
Hiss
Scuttle
Pop
Splash
Sizzle
Drip
Boom

page 66 — Ancient Adventure

```
H S I R U E R M N R H A P I H T H
I G U A P E A P A K H O R H C S C
E H I M S S S O H O I S R O T T H
R E P S P H L C M A R N P U I R H
O O I E I A C L S U R O G H S K T
G G A S P P O E A F M A H T I E Y
L U U P I A S O Y E R M O U U N O
Y R P T H P I P I X M M I H O T X
P E S Y P Y R A M I D C O F U R P
H P A S C R I T R M P G S R Y E H
I O T A R U S R R L I G I Z A I G
C A R L A S R A C A S I T R M Y R
```

page 67 — Awesome!

```
E P L E N C P O M T A N
C I L A T I E M O A O C
L R A Z N W U W I J P I
E R E C H J C A A M C C
M L N O A C E L H A E H
F I E L E I S L C H H I
E E L O E R R O Z A L C
H O T S A E E F M L R H
R T D S L R C C C R E D
T L H E S E L H C R D E
T H A U Z F L I C W E I
I H A M E A L N W P E T
E M U E L O I A I U M Z
F C P I C C H U H O E A
A O E Z A S O P R H R A
L E H I N R L E E R U O
R E I C P E T R A E O H
```

page 68 — Word Magician

MILD – MIND – WIND – WAND – HAND

SPICY – SPACE – PLACE – PLANT – BLAND

page 69 — Total Opposites

ACROSS
2. Winter
4. Asleep
7. Easy

DOWN
1. Short
2. Whisper
3. Empty
5. Sunny
6. Over

page 70 — Cool Capitals!

```
D J O L T O L A I P A Y
O L N I T O P E K A D U
D E N V E R L S U O L E
S A N N A P O L I S U Y
A S L B O N L O L J P T
A H O N O L U L U H N
A U O L T S I T B N O L
I A T L A N T A E E E N
L S P A O A E O N A N O
V N U L T S N E N U I A
N M N B T H E U T S X N
O A H A M V I S N U P A
I E Y O L Y M P I A L
N S N T A L P E L D A S
N O L I L E P N L H A I
A N K P N O N I O Y A P
```

page 71 — Main Hub

Washington, D.C. Tokyo Amman Kuala Lumpur

Addis Ababa Suva New Delhi Ottawa

Lisbon Buenos Aires San Salvador Paris

Dhaka Wellington Nairobi

page 72 — What Does It Mean?

1. A
2. B
3. B
4. A

5. A
6. A
7. B
8. B

page 73 — At the Castle!

```
R R R D U N G E O N A G E T H
R G E R R R N T R E A O S A T R
C C T A K O R A G L G S T L E
G R D W N E F O A E E T R R E
G E R B I G O G R A D E G L T
U N T R G T R T G A F R R U S
E E I H A T R A R N D D Y G
T L I D T E R D E A R M T Y T
R L W G N U E G A E R O E T T
O A T E T R S T O T E A C R U
S T A R O U S Y O Y A T A R R
G I D R W O G T I N L I L T R
T O G R E L N T U R R E T N E
T N G R R O I O A R E O E A I
L N N I E O E L O R R T U N F
```

page 74 — That's a Wrap!

DIRECTOR
ACTING
FILMING
BIG SCREEN
CUT

RED CARPET
BOX OFFICE
HOLLYWOOD
SCRIPT

page 75 — Crack the Code

The word "movie" is from the term "moving picture"!

page 76 — Go Greek

```
H O U E T R E O O H E B
S S H I I S O E E A R E
N A E T T E L E T E O E
O P R R A C H I L L E S
S U C C N S A T T S O O
A L U C S A L S Z E M H
O T L P E Z O O P E P A
E P E G A S U S L B A S
O O S C U R A T H E N A
S S S R O T T A S S D P
U S S E A P S E I O O O
E T L A E H S R M C R L
M Y T H O L O G Y I A L
E U A L I D H Z M T S O
G Z U P P O S E I D O N
N C E R B E R U S H S T
E U L U E A R S H A O E
```

page 77 — The Myth, The Legend

```
T L L G M F I L P F A E O A O T F
I A L N A W O N Y M G M L O G A R
F I I W I L E Y P E U F T E N F A
I U L F N C F A I R Y R A B O R C
B N F T M R R O H M D L W I E L C
G E L G G A D E C A H U W G T O U
N N F I D R N R R I A O R F R O N
E N O O M C F A A D L C T O O E I
F M P M O F R Y E G R R I O L D C
F M A C E N T A U R O P A T L N O
F D L E P R E C H A U N E A G H R
U N E W E R E W O L F A E L R T N
```

page 78 — Play Ball!

ACROSS
3. Hoop
7. Birdie
8. Referee
9. Bowling

DOWN
1. Soccer
2. Racket
4. Baseball
5. Whistle
6. Superbowl
7. Beach

page 79 — Rock On!

T U D E: Duet
G T A U I R: Guitar
N A B D: Band
O N I P A: Piano
R E N O C C T: Concert
S H O C U R: Chorus
D A I R O: Radio
N O S G: Song

page 80 — Backward and Forward

```
D K S A O A N D S R A E K P V
A R N N O O K O R K V N A K O
S E E S O L Y A O A E R D P A
T R K F R R A R T N E A O A R
P E D A E L B V A O R S N R A
E O O K Y R I L T D T Y K E B
O N R E A A B E O R O N O S S
R A N O E R K V R K E T K A A
E A I A R I D E E D E O N K R
F E D R S S R L P E P E R N E
F R S A E O B K A A F O E Y E
E T I D R E P A N R A O E E E
N P T E A I R L K E E L D E F
K O S O T A D T E R E N A V T
A N B O A E B B R F B R D R F
```

page 81 — Word Magician

TYPE – TAPE – TAKE – MAKE – CAKE

SLOW – BROW – BRIM – BEAM – HEAR

page 82 — Down the Rabbit Hole

ACROSS
2. Rabbit
7. Underground
9. Meerkat
10. Tunnels

DOWN
1. Chipmunk
3. Hole
4. Grasslands
5. Australia
6. Otter
8. Den

page 83 — Coral Chorus

```
R I L H F K R G R M H O O T P S A
W S A N M I R A G C R C A U A R A
A L Y O M I R R H G T I P R R O C
I E P P R D R A G O N A I T R O U
C F C O O L N T F B R F A L O E G
H O L G C I R R A Y T A C E T A A
S R O I O O R R B O P W H E F S T
O R W O R U I I L B W I O O I S O
O G N Y I N C N G E A C U C S A O
O O F I R A G S R E U N O B H R L
N S I R S A G W I O C T O P U S C
C P S U E W F I R E W O R M O R A
P S H A R K C C B O A A S I N S O
```

page 84 — Slithery Snakes

```
C C T P S R A E R R G E S T S
T E V P Y R A E R N A A N C A
R E P R E I N C I S A I N O R
A I R C N G A O N R C N T P E
A N R S O T A B P A O A N P E
P O A S H E N R P I N T C E E
Y I T C A K A A T R S H R R O
T G T A O I O P R E T S P H P
H E L T R N O T A V R C V E E
O C E K A G D A T N I K S A Y
N R S S H S O A T C C P T D I
R D N T P N K D A N T O E E R
K R A C O A R K P O O H P R N
E A K C E K T K P P R R B E C
N P E I R E P H E G A R A R S
```

page 85 — Lizard Blizzard

```
O O G G S N A G N K A N E M N
H E A S N C C H A M E L E O N
R S N N D A I A C K C N U N S
E U O K O E C R E R L A D I O
G N K I C U E A E G M O R T Z
O G S G U S O T H N O N A O E
E A R U S K G O E A D U G R O
T Z H A U I E D K C A E O C N
N E R N E N C N O S N L N A C
I R S A O K K R K A G E T A N
O O N D N M O N S T E R S R U
A O A N U C M U T A T N E K O
O N M E N G R O O E G A N S H
K R S O C S N E E N L S E K L
N E A R R G G N O R K E T U E
```

page 86 — Beach Days

ACROSS
3. Lifeguard
4. Popsicle
7. Vacation
8. Towel
10. Bucket
11. Surfer
12. Crab

DOWN
1. Boardwalk
2. Jellyfish
4. Pacific
5. Saltwater
6. Castle
9. Sunscreen

page 87 — Word Magician

LIME – TIME – TIDE – TIDY – TINY

WAVE – WALK – BACK – PICK – PARK

page 88 — Solar System Scramble

C E R M U R Y: Mercury

S N E V U: Venus

R A T H E: Earth

A R M S: Mars

P R U T J I E: Jupiter

N U R A S T: Saturn

S A R U N U: Uranus

E N U P E N T: Neptune

page 89 — Space Quiz

1. D
2. A
3. B
4. A
5. B

page 90 — Word Whiz

```
I S N G I G G L E T O C Q U T
V T Y C O O N A E R L O U U B
I L N T E U O T I L I A Q N E
L E T I L L R T Y O N L C N A
L K S C S E Q U I N A K K N O
A A G H G Y B I T K G O O W B
I E I L T T G S N A S A E H I
N U O U O T N I N N B I G I I
I L N F N U B I B G R A I R L
I G N N U I K Q L I R G L E C
B A C O G C A S C K A I I A C
N V O I T R T T C N N O I L O
V O N Q O I I U I N L I T W
T G U I L V R Q O W G A L N I
E O E Y I I G O T N U A C W U
```

page 91 — Word Whiz Quiz

QUACK: A sound made by a duck

WHIRL: To move in a circle

FICTION: A made-up story

GIGGLE: To laugh lightly and in a silly way

RUTABAGA: A round yellow vegetable

VILLAIN: The evil or bad character in a story

SEQUIN: A small shiny circle, often sewn onto clothing

TYCOON: A rich and powerful businessperson

page 92 — High Count

```
L L O T O L T O L H T C
D O S O A D R O T G B N
O C L U L O I N O O A M
R T D N B I L L I O N T
N I O E O L L I O G O H
N L D I O O I A L O A O
D L O L I S O B L L M U
M I L L I O N I U O H S
I O T P M L N I P L N A
N N S E P T I L L I O N
N O O N I D T I G L O D
Q U A D R I L L I O N S
I I O G N E O O I T C L
N L L T C L I R O L L T
O R L I L E P A O T S L
O L M N L N N S I L I B
O O N I N L I O N L I I
```

page 93 — Shape It Up!

 Triangle

 Hexagon

 Octagon

 Rectangle

Square

Semicircle

Oval

Star

Heart

page 94 — Switch It!

SLOWER: Flower
LOG: Dog
DAMP: Lamp
TEN: Hen
LAND: Hand
TELL: Bell
REAL: Seal
FREE: Tree
HOOK: Book

page 95 — Super Sleuth

LADEP: Fake
CABOOSE: Real
AMUSING: Real
PASTURE: Real
MANSION: Real
SNOOP: Real
ASTERISK: Real
FENCELET: Fake
KHAKI: Real
PLONSKIRTING: Fake
GRICKLE: Fake

page 96 — Slice of Paradise

E H E E C S: Cheese
E O I P P P E R N: Pepperoni
N O N O I: Onion
A P I P N E L P E: Pineapple
L O V I E S: Olives
S U M O H O R M: Mushroom
L A S A M I: Salami
R E E P P P S: Peppers

page 97 — I Scream, You Scream

```
E I V I E A O B A N R C C E L
T P M A A O I R E R T L V I T
R I N T N E A M A S Y E S O Y
T S P E R I C K C C I R S O C
I T O T A M L T L R T S B B A
K A E H R P A L O T E S R U C
E C M I N T O E A R Y A L T O
H H H R E P N L A M C P M T S
T I R O C K Y I I Q K H T E R
B O L H C S R E Y T E A O R E
R A S H C O O K I E A L A H O
E Y T C O A L S V B C N O N O
C Y O T B E A A S I N E L A T
Y R E P E C A N T Y O B P V E
E E L S T R A W B E R R Y I O
```

page 98 — Rhyme Time!

POWER
CARE
DIME
TOWN
HANDLE
CUDDLE
LIGHT
PEN

page 99 — The Name of the Game

1. D   4. B
2. C   5. D
3. B

page 100 — Catching Prey

```
O L A A E T O W I T U O A O U
O L E E N E A N I F L I T D E
L O L A L T A N O R I D A F E
U E R A R A R O A E F L R A E
R A O O Y T E F I L L W A L R
O A T N E A A O O O C A N C R
D O E N O I U R C C W N U N O
E L T A Y A O W L A C L L O L
W O R C R O C O D I L E A N H
A W U T R B T L C C A N R L Y
R Y T A I A O F A T A E C L E
Y F U C A G N R O O A C T A N
F L Y E D E E N C R H B I T A
R A C H A L N R E A L A L W Y
```

page 101 — Word Magician

TRY – CRY – DRY – DAY – HAY

SEAT – FEET – FEAR – FOUR – LOUD

page 102 — I Feel Happy!

```
G L A D L B C H E E R F U L J
L L L B L I S S F U L E D Y U I
L U I O D Y D L E L H A P P Y
I A D U C E S F C R L A S O E
B L D D O E X C I T E D R S A
E O T I R G G I D D Y R O A P
X G P Y I R B E R L F E L U H
R L L Y Y I H T L T F A B X E
L M H H E U L L L E F H L A G
L L E X F F H E M Y P J E E E
L O S R Y I A R L R C O D Y L
L T A B R G F E E D D L L Y D
A H S A U Y I U L Y I L Y Y S
D T O A H S E E E B I Y X E L
G R L S I O T G P F Y S L H T
```

page 103 — Seeing Red

```
I D I D I M R D I G I E M D E
E U G B G G S N E D A R N I D
A N G U U A U S E M G A A Y E
N B B I A G E T I E O E S S U
A G A O G F O E E E I O O O N
A N R G I O U A N O O S N D O
U B S E D L F M C R O S S O N
D I G O D F I I G A D B O N
F E U N I G N N O N G G M A S
U G U D U N I G G R G T E A D
R F A I C M R O O C O L U D D
I O R R G S K R A T R O N R A
O U T R A G E D M S E E E U I
U R A E N E D E E D G A E E L
S E I I N G A N N O Y E D F O
```

page 104 — My Gang

```
M O D R W S W A R M O C
R O P C M C A S C A D C
A C S C H O O L I P I O
P S N P Y L I D P P E Y
A R M Y R O P A R A D E
R S I A E N S R A R P R
A A I D C Y P O D L A A
H A A O E K R K T I K R
O P A R P C M H A A A K
I O P M O A R A O M L P
R M E R E S S K A E L A
V E D A M S E P Y N N M
R W H R Y H E A V T E P
H E M M C I O C S A O O
R L A A S V O K C K K D
N R C A R E P S P E P R
H T P P M R Y C I P O E
```

page 105 — Group Effort

SWARM: Bees
COLONY: Ants
ARMY: Frogs
PACK: Wolves
SCHOOL: Fish
SMACK: Jellyfish

PRIDE: Lions
PARLIAMENT: Owls
SHIVER: Sharks
POD: Whales
PARADE: Elephants

page 106 — Olympic Gold!

```
M M I G H T S A R E T M G S A
W N N Y Y T A K R E L E K H N
S H S W I M M I N G E C A T A
L C J O A T N T E N N I S B A
O N M L C Y M A J N H R A S A
G R T A L C S A S U A A E S M
H R N R C M E S K T D O R T G
T R N C O Y K R O I I O T E N
S G A H N R A G U K E C A N I
D S C E S A R A R I B T S W K
R S G R L M A S K A T I N G I
G A O Y I R T Y I E S A S R A
M R B A S K E T B A L L O M K
M S A E T M M A R A T H O N E
I I N R H W M M S N S S I I Y
```

page 107 — Welcome to the Museum!

```
L E G W L A L R E A O W I N P
L O H E A I M A P O E N P L U
T A E T R U G N L E C Y I T S
G E P L I N L W L T E T N P O
C O S M R D E I A S P S A S C
L P L U O N S E K E D L N M A
K A O D E M J C L U T O R A N
P I U S A R C O P H A G U S T
G N A K L A T U W O I S R K W
I T Y E G I Y O S S D M N O U
P I L L L S C U L P T U R E E
G N T E I F W J A O W G O C U
K G L T L T T J E W E L R Y H
S P A O E D G W E A P O N H T
I A L N C F O S S I L D S A F
```

page 108 — Find the Animal

SLUM: Slug

BAM: Bat

HIPPY: Hippo

GOAL: Goat

SHARP: Shark

PIN: Pig

SHEET: Sheep

YAP: Yak

WORD: Worm

NEWS: Newt

page 109 — Birthday Party!

```
L A R P L A L L D S T A I A P G P
B N S N E N R Y S R K O N A C O P
N T T V H C A K E E O B V E E O R
Y P R S N D M E L P N A I Y L D E
E E E P C E R M N I T L T V E Y S
P C A N D L E S O S L L A L B I E
P O M R E A A O R C G O T O R T N
A R E H H A T L R A K O I O A S T
R T R P A H E I N L Y N O L T O S
T O S N R P A M A N G S N N I T A
Y E E S R A P T S E O C E A O G A
L C R E A M Y Y N E L R D S N Y L
```

page 110 — Engineer That!

ACROSS

3. Hammer
5. Excavator
6. Hard hat
7. Dump truck
8. Wheelbarrow
10. Drill

DOWN

1. Bridge
2. Cement
4. Jackhammer
9. Worksite

page 111 — Career Day

NURSE
FIREFIGHTER
FARMER
DIRECTOR
ARTIST
SCIENTIST

DESIGNER
TEACHER
PRESIDENT
WRITER
BUILDER
CHEF

PICTURE CREDITS

The publisher would like to thank the following for permission to reproduce their images. The publisher apologizes for any omissions and will be pleased to make any corrections in future editions.

l = left; r = right; t = top; b = bottom; c = center; u = upper

p. 10 seamartini/iStockphoto; p. 39 filo/iStockphoto; p. 41 Shendart/iStockphoto; p. 42 Volodymyr Kotoshchuk/iStockphoto; pp. 46-47 JakeOlimb/iStockphoto; p. 65 tl irmetov/iStockphoto, p. 65 clt Ekaterina Vakhrameeva/iStockphoto; p. 65 clb Redlio Designs/iStockphoto; p. 65 bl1 GoodGnom/iStockphoto; p. 65 bl2 cpuga/iStockphoto; p. 65 crt RobinOlimb/iStockphoto; p. 65 crb kristina-s/iStockphoto; p. 65 br siraanamwong/iStockphoto; p. 71 pop_jop/iStockphoto p. 79 Sissoupitch/iStockphoto; p. 88 drmakkoy /iStockphoto; p. 92 jamesjames2541/iStockphoto; p. 96 tl Irina Gubanova/iStockphoto; p. 96 clt Irina Gubanova/iStockphoto; p. 96 clb trigubova/iStockphoto; p. 96 bl trigubova/iStockphoto; p. 96 tr trigubova/iStockphoto; p. 96 crt trigubova/iStockphoto; p. 96 crb trigubova/iStockphoto; p. 96 br Irina Gubanova/iStockphoto; p. 108 (slug and worm) Alfadanz/iStockphoto; (bat) pixitive/iStockphoto; (hippo, goat, pig, and sheep) Macrovector/iStockphoto; (yak) AlonzoDesign/iStockphoto; (newt) mariaflaya/iStockphoto; p. 109 Tetiana Lazunova/iStockphoto; p. 110 filo/iStockphoto.